MINISTERING THROUGH SPIRITUAL GIFTS

BY

CHARLES F. STANLEY

THOMAS NELSON
Since 1798

NASHVILLE   DALLAS   MEXICO CITY   RIO DE JANEIRO

Published in Nashville, Tennessee, by Thomas Nelson, Inc.

G𝖢B

Editing, layout, and design by Gregory C. Benoit Publishing, Old Mystic, CT

Scripture quotations are from THE NEW KING JAMES VERSION. Copyright © 1979, 1980, 1982, Thomas Nelson, Inc., Publishers.

9781418541286

2 3 4 5 6 14 13 12 11

Contents

Approaching the Motivational Gifts

A number of books are available today that help a person understand their individual talents and abilities and learn more about how to use them to achieve success. This book is unlike them in two ways: First, this book is intended for Bible study—it is not a stand-alone book. Second, this book is intended to help you discover the *spiritual* gift(s) God has given you and built into your very personality so that you may use this gift for the success of the body of Christ as a whole—not for your own personal success. The intent for using any spiritual gift is not personal gain, but the building up of others within the church.

These gifts are spiritual in nature, so they are not going to be readily understood by those who do not have a personal relationship with Jesus Christ. All of what we come to understand about our spiritual motivational gifts and their use is revealed to us by the Holy Spirit. Therefore, this study should be undertaken by those who are believers in Jesus Christ and who desire both to know and to use their gifts effectively.

In our study, we will use the terms "ministry gifts" and "motivational gifts" interchangeably. These are the spiritual gifts that motivate us to minister to others. They are ministry gifts in that they are always intended to build up others in the body of Christ.

This book can be used by you alone or by several people in a small-group study. At various times, you will be asked to relate to the material in one of these four ways:

1. *What new insights have you gained?* Make notes about any insights you may have. Record them in your Bible or in a separate journal. As

you reflect back over your insights, you are likely to see how God has moved in your life.

2. *Have you ever had a similar experience?* Each of us approaches the Bible from a unique background—our own particular set of relationships and experiences. Our experiences do not make the Bible true—the Word of God is truth regardless of our opinion about it. It is important, however, to share our experiences in order to see how God's truth can be applied to human lives.

3. *How do you feel about the material presented?* Emotional responses do not give validity to the Word of God, nor should we trust our emotions as a gauge for our faith. In small-group Bible study, however, it is good for participants to express their emotions. The Holy Spirit often communicates with us through this unspoken language.

4. *In what way do you feel challenged to respond or act?* God's Word may cause you to feel inspired or challenged to change something in your life. Take the challenge seriously and find ways of acting upon it. If God reveals to you a particular need that He wants *you* to address, take that as "marching orders" from God. God is expecting you to *do* something with the challenge that He has just given you.

Start and conclude your Bible study sessions in prayer. Ask God to give you spiritual eyes to see and spiritual ears to hear. As you conclude your study, ask the Lord to seal what you have learned so that you will never forget it. Ask Him to help you grow into the fullness of the stature of Christ Jesus.

As you move forward, make sure to keep the Bible at the center of your study. A genuine Bible study stays focused on God's Word and promotes a growing faith and closer walk with the Holy Spirit in each person who participates.

Lesson 1

God's Special Gift to You

─────── ❧ **In This Lesson** ❧ ───────

Learning: What exactly are motivational gifts?

Growing: Where do motivational gifts come from?

───────── ∞ ─────────

Do you know your innate spiritual gift? Have you identified the most important gift that God has given to you for the purposes of ministry in His name? Every Christian has been given a spiritual gift from God—a gift designed to be used as part of the body of Christ and for the purpose of assisting others. Every believer receives these gifts at the moment of accepting Jesus Christ as personal Savior. They are intended to be the main avenue through which a person ministers to others within the church as a whole.

I refer to these gifts as "motivational gifts," for they are intended to *motivate* us toward service. They are gifts that compel and inspire us to act in specific ways. They are the particular bent that we have to serve God's people and others whom we desire to see become Christians. I believe it is vitally important to our personal spiritual lives, as well as to the overall spiritual life of a church, for us to recognize these gifts, to encourage their proper use in the church, and to encourage one another as we exercise our gifts.

The Nature of Motivational Gifts

Several things about these gifts are vital for us to acknowledge at the outset of our study:

1. Every person has received a "motivational" gift. Some people may seem gifted with a number of them, but one of the seven gifts covered in this study is going to be dominant in a person's life. The gift is resident from a person's birth, and it becomes fully operative for its God-given purposes when that person is born again.

2. The motivational gifts are intended to be used in the church for building up God's people. Each of the motivational gifts covered in this study may be employed "in the flesh." When this happens, disaster generally follows. The misuse of the gifts is actually counterproductive to the work that the Holy Spirit desires to do in us individually and in the church as a whole. We must rely completely upon the Holy Spirit to assist us in the use of our motivational gifts.

3. We are commanded by God to use these gifts. Peter wrote to the church, "As each one has received a gift, minister it to one another, as good stewards of the manifold grace of God" (1 Pet. 4:10).

4. The motivational gifts reside in the believer. These gifts are built into a person's personality. They are who we are in the church. Other gifts are identified in the New Testament as residing in the Holy Spirit—such gifts operate "as the Spirit wills" and may be manifested in any believer's life from time to time. (See 1 Corinthians 12:8–11 for such a list.) The motivational gifts, however, do not come and go in the believer's life—they are permanent. For example, a person does not manifest the motivational gift of prophecy for six months, and then shift to a motivational gift of service for the next three years, and then shift to another gift. Motivational gifts span the course of a person's life. They may manifest in slightly different ways, in different situations, with varying degrees of intensity, but the identity of the gift remains intact and is unchangeable.

5. We each have a responsibility to discover and use our spiritual gifts. The more we learn about our spiritual gifts, the greater the responsibility we have to use them for the benefit of others. The first thing we must recognize is that we have a motivational gift given to us by God; then we must recognize which of the seven gifts have been given. That is a major step for many believers who have never considered themselves to be "gifted" by God in any particular way. Let me repeat again: *you* have been given a spiritual motivational gift by God. *You* bear this as part of your identity. *You* are responsible for identifying your gift, developing it, and then using it for the glory of God. The more you use your motivational gift, the more you will grow in it, and the more the Holy Spirit will be able to use you in it.

⌘ Do you know what your motivational gift is? If so, how are you using it at present?

⌘ If you are not sure what your motivational gift is, make a list below of things that you're naturally good at. Return to this list after completing this study to help you identify your gift.

No Spectators Allowed

The church was never designed by God to include spectators. Every person within the church—which is the greater Body of Christ—is expected to be vibrantly alive and active, each one using his motivational gift at all times and in as many situations as possible, and each believer being open to use by the Holy Spirit as He wills in the manifestation of other spiritual gifts.

So many people in the church today are sitting on the sidelines watching others take active roles. It's been estimated that eighty percent of those who attend church regularly watch the other twenty percent do the work. That is detrimental to the individuals who are inactive, to the individuals who are active, and to the work of the Lord as a whole. It certainly is not God's desire or design. God desires that each person be active in the use of his gifts so that the following might occur:

    ∝ Each person may grow more and more into the fullness of what God intended in his life from the moment of creation.

    ∝ The work within the church may be evenly distributed so that no one reaches the state of overload or burn out.

    ∝ The work of the church as a whole may be effective, vibrant, and balanced.

This study is designed to help you understand the spiritual gifts and to help you identify your own particular gift, motivating you toward the use of that gift. I believe that two things will happen as you understand who you are in Jesus Christ and what your identity is within the Body of Christ. First, I believe that you are going to be excited about your identity and the ways in which God desires to use you. Second, I believe that you are going to be challenged to develop your gift and employ it to the best of your ability. God has many special rewards reserved for those who employ their motivational ministry gifts to the best of their abilities—don't miss out on them.

 Have you accepted Jesus Christ as your personal Savior? If so, you have received a motivational gift for use in the body of Christ. If not, what is preventing you from accepting God's gift of salvation right now?

> As each one has received a gift, minister it to one another, as good stewards of the manifold grace of God.
>
> —1 Peter 4:10

 What does it mean to minister your gifts "one to another"? How is this done? Why is it important?

 What does Peter mean by "the manifold grace of God"? What does God's grace have to do with your spiritual gifts?

❧ Today and Tomorrow ❧

TODAY: EVERY CHRISTIAN IS GIVEN A MOTIVATIONAL GIFT BY THE HOLY SPIRIT, INTENDED FOR USE IN BUILDING UP OTHERS.

TOMORROW: I WILL SPEND TIME IN PRAYER AND REFLECTION THIS WEEK, ASKING THE LORD TO SHOW ME WHAT MOTIVATIONAL GIFT HE HAS GIVEN ME.

LESSON 2

An Overview of the Ministry Gifts

---— ❧ **In This Lesson** ❧ ———

LEARNING: WHAT DOES IT MEAN TO BE IN THE "BODY OF CHRIST"?

GROWING: HOW CAN I USE MY SPIRITUAL GIFT WITHIN THAT BODY?

———— ∞ ————

The motivational gifts were identified by the apostle Paul in his letter to the Romans. He prefaced his definition of the seven motivational gifts, however, with an important admonition: "For as we have many members in one body, but all the members do not have the same function, so we, being many, are one body in Christ, and individually members of one another" (Rom. 12:4, 5).

At the very outset of our study of the motivational gifts, I want you to focus on Paul's statement that "all the members do not have the same function" and yet all are "one body in Christ." We can be different, and yet be united! We have different gifts and roles to play within the church, and yet there are many things that we share in common. As concerned as Paul was about our individual gifts, he was equally concerned that the church regard itself as a whole and function as a whole.

~ Recall a situation in your life in which diversity and unity were both present. What enabled people to be different yet united together?

~ When have you seen division caused by people with different skills, aptitudes, or goals? What caused the division? How might people have become more unified together?

The apostle Paul also wrote about our diversity and unity to the Corinthians:

> There are diversities of gifts, but the same Spirit. There are differences of ministries, but the same Lord. And there are diversities of activities, but it is the same God who works all in all. But the manifestation of the Spirit is given to each one for the profit of all . . . For as the body is one and has many members, but all the members of that one body, being many, are one body, so also is Christ. For by one Spirit we were all baptized into one body—whether Jews or Greeks, whether slaves or free—and have all been made to drink into one Spirit. For in fact the body is not one member but many.
>
> If the foot should say, "Because I am not a hand, I am not of the body," is it therefore not of the body? And if the ear should say, "Because I am not an eye, I am not of the body," is it therefore not of the body? If the whole body were an eye,

where would be the hearing? If the whole were hearing, where would be the smelling? But now God has set the members, each one of them, in the body just as He pleased. And if they were all one member, where would the body be? . . .

But God composed the body, having given greater honor to that part which lacks it, that there should be no schism in the body, but that the members should have the same care for one another. And if one member suffers, all the members suffer with it; or if one member is honored, all the members rejoice with it.

—1 Cor. 12:4–7, 12–19, 24–26

❧ Why does Paul use the human body as a metaphor in these passages? What does it mean that "the body is not one member but many"? How does this apply to spiritual gifts?

❧ What does Paul mean when he says "that there should be no schism in the body"? What are schisms? What causes them? How can they be avoided?

11

Seven Gifts Given for Ministry Purposes

It is against the backdrop of a unified body that the apostle Paul identified seven motivational gifts:

> Having then gifts differing according to the grace that is given to us, let us use them: if prophecy, let us prophesy in proportion to our faith; or ministry, let us use it in our ministering; he who teaches, in teaching; he who exhorts, in exhortation; he who gives, with liberality; he who leads, with diligence; he who shows mercy, with cheerfulness.
>
> —Romans 12:6–8

Note clearly the seven gifts that Paul identifies:

1. Prophecy
2. Ministering, which may also be called Service
3. Teaching
4. Exhortation
5. Giving
6. Leading, which may also be called Administration or Organization
7. Mercy

Paul further states in this passage that each person has one of these gifts "according to the grace that is given to us" (v. 6). God is the giver of the gifts, and through His Holy Spirit He is the one who helps us identify, develop, and use our gifts. These are not gifts that we "work up" or choose for ourselves. They are a gift from God to us. We must recognize how we are made, embrace our own gift, and then seek to grow in it.

Below are seven verses that relate to each of these seven motivational gifts. Some of the verses are in contexts other than spiritual gifts, such as that of eldership or the fruit of the Spirit. Nevertheless, the principles described for each gift will serve as an overview introduction to how that gift should be used. As you read through these passages, recognize that motivational gifts are to be used in all contexts of your life: at home, in one-on-one encounters, and on the job—but *especially* in the church.

    Prophecy: "Pursue love, and desire spiritual gifts, but especially that you may prophesy" (1 Corinthians 14:1).

    Ministering or Serving: "For you, brethren, have been called to liberty; only do not use liberty as an opportunity for the flesh, but through love serve one another" (Galatians 5:13).

    Teaching: "For this reason I have sent Timothy to you, who is my beloved and faithful son in the Lord, who will remind you of my ways in Christ, as I teach everywhere in every church" (1 Corinthians 4:17).

    Exhorting: "Beware, brethren, lest there be in any of you an evil heart of unbelief in departing from the living God; but exhort one another daily, while it is called 'Today,' lest any of you be hardened through the deceitfulness of sin" (Hebrews 3:12, 13).

    Giving: "Give, and it will be given to you: good measure, pressed down, shaken together, and running over will be put into your bosom. For with the same measure that you use, it will be measured back to you" (Luke 6:38).

    Leading: "A bishop then must be . . . one who rules his own house well, having his children in submission with all reverence (for if a man does not know how to rule his own house, how will he take care of the church of God?)" (1 Timothy 3:2, 4, 5).

    Mercy: "Therefore, as the elect of God, holy and beloved, put on tender mercies, kindness, humility, meekness, longsuffering" (Colossians 3:12).

What themes do you find in all these verses concerning the proper use of spiritual gifts?

How is each of these gifts used, in practical terms?

Prophecy:

Serving:

Teaching:

Exhorting:

Giving:

Leading:

Mercy:

For as the body is one and has many members, but all the members of that one body, being many, are one body, so also is Christ. For by one Spirit we were all baptized into one body.

—1 Corinthians 12:12, 13

☙ Picture yourself walking. How do different parts of your body participate in that activity? What do your arms do? Your hips? Your eyes?

☙ How is this a metaphor for the proper use of spiritual gifts? How might the seven gifts listed above work together in some single ministry?

Discovering Your Particular Gift

If you are not able to identify your own motivational gift at this point, do not be alarmed. In the lessons that follow, you will have ample opportunity to zero in on your specific gift. Recognize at this point that there are several reasons that Christians don't recognize their own gifts.

1. They may have a "cloudy" relationship with God. They may not have accepted Jesus Christ as their Savior. They may not know that, as a believer in Jesus Christ, they have been indwelt by the Holy Spirit or that they have been given a ministry gift. They may be unsure about their position in Jesus Christ. If any of these issues is relevant to your life, I encourage you to take action. Accept Jesus Christ as your Savior. Invite the Holy Spirit to guide you, and remind yourself daily of your reliance upon Him to teach you and guide. Study God's Word to discover your position in Jesus Christ. (See the *InTouch* Bible study, *Living in His Sufficiency*.)

2. They may not be involved in service to others. Much of what we discover about ourselves, and particularly about our ministry gift, is learned only as we attempt to help others.

3. They may be attempting to imitate another person—perhaps someone they admire or the person who led them to Christ. As long as we are trying to copy the ministry gift of another person, we will not be in a position to recognize and develop our own gift from God.

4. They may have failed to recognize the motivation for their own actions. Many people never ask why they do or say certain things. Discovering one's motivational gift requires a certain degree or introspection and self-examination.

5. They may be confused about the difference between ministry and gift. Ministry is a specific act of service to others. Working with the children's choir and feeding the homeless are two examples of ministry. A ministry gift is the motivation that leads us to engage in a particular facet of ministry. For example, the person who is involved in the children's choir may have the gift of leading—such a person is likely to administer and organize the program, and may very well be the choirmaster. Another person involved in the children's choir may have a gift of service—such a person may be the one who makes sure that the choir robes are clean and pressed, or that refreshments are available to the children after the rehearsals.

6. They may have a false understanding that only full-time clergy and staff members in a church are gifted or qualified for ministry. The ministry gifts are given to all members of the church. Every person has been gifted and is commanded by God to use his or her gift. Church roles are identified elsewhere in Scripture as apostles, prophets, evangelists, pastors, and teachers. Even within the church roles, a person will have a tendency to gravitate toward a particular motivational gift.

✍ Which of the above misconceptions have you struggled with? How has such thinking hindered your spiritual gift?

✍ What will you do this week to correct those ways of thinking? How will you use your gift in service to the Lord?

How the Gifts Work Together

The motivational gifts are designed to work together, to complement each other and to be joined together in productive ways that bring benefit to the whole body of believers. As we develop and exercise our motivational gifts, we bring refinement and balance to the body as a whole. Three key words were emphasized by Jesus, Paul, and other New Testament writers regarding the way we treat one another and minister to one another:

> **Love:** We are to treat others with love at all times. Love must be our attitude, the tone of our voice, the purpose for our actions, and the goal that we seek in all relationships.
>
> **Humility:** We are to treat others with respect, gentleness, and patience.
>
> **Peace:** We are to create an overall atmosphere of peace and reconciliation within the church. Ministry gifts are never intended to divide God's people, but rather to heal, restore, nurture, unify, and build up God's people in a strong and vibrant whole.

The exercise of gifts without love and humility results in our coming across as "sounding brass or clanging cymbal"—obnoxious sounds that interrupt and bring discord. Love, however, builds up and brings peace. Any exercise of our motivational gifts without love brings no benefit to us or others. For our ministry gifts to be effective and to be a blessing, we must choose to love, we must work for peace, and we must remain humble in our relationships with others.

When we use our motivational gifts in godly ways, we experience minimum weariness and maximum effectiveness. It is as we develop and use our ministry gifts that we find deep inner satisfaction and contentment: the purpose for our life is fulfilled, and we have a great sense of meaning.

This is My commandment, that you love one another as I have loved you. Greater love has no one than this, than to lay down one's life for his friends.

—John 15:12, 13

≈ What does it mean, in practical terms, to love others as Jesus loves you?

≈ How might exercising your spiritual gift involve laying down your life for others (either literally or figuratively)?

≈ Today and Tomorrow ≈

TODAY: THE LORD HAS GIVEN ME A MINISTRY GIFT, AND I MUST LEARN TO USE IT TO BRING STRENGTH AND HEALTH TO THE BODY OF CHRIST.

TOMORROW: I WILL SPEND TIME THIS WEEK ASKING THE LORD TO SHOW ME HOW TO USE MY GIFT IN SERVICE TO HIM.

LESSON 3

The Gift of Prophecy

──────── ❧ **In This Lesson** ❧ ────────

LEARNING: DOES A PROPHET FORETELL FUTURE EVENTS?

GROWING: WHAT FUNCTION DOES A PROPHET HAVE IN THE CHURCH TODAY?

──────── ∞ ────────

Do you find that you can't remain quiet or sit still when you are hearing a lie or are in the presence of evil? Do you have a clear-cut understanding of what God considers to be right and wrong? You may have been given the gift of prophecy.

Prophets are those who speak the truth. Many people have an understanding of prophecy as "foretelling the future," but the more general meaning for this term in the Bible is "forth-telling"—proclaiming the principles of God which are true now and forever. The genuine prophet of God *must* speak the truth—he cannot remain quiet in the face of a lie or any form of deceit, or in the face of an error against God's Word or God's nature. The prophet is very often a person who sees things in black-and-white, right-or-wrong terms. He has a strong motivation to set things right or to get the church back on the right track, and speaks boldly in the presence of injustice.

Peter functioned in the role of the prophet. As the focus for this study, we'll identify the general nature of the gift of prophecy, and in each case we'll look at an instance in which Peter manifested this gift.

1. The gift of prophecy leads a person to confront evil, hypocrisy, error, and false conclusions. On the day of Pentecost, the followers of Jesus were accused by onlookers of being drunk with wine—and it was Peter who took action.

> But Peter, standing up with the eleven, raised his voice and said to them, "Men of Judea and all who dwell in Jerusalem, let this be known to you, and heed my words. For these are not drunk, as you suppose, since it is only the third hour of the day. But this is what was spoken by the prophet Joel. . . .
>
> —Acts 2:14–16

2. The gift of prophecy often reveals the character and motives of others, especially those motives that are deceitful or hypocritical. Ananias and Sapphira conspired to lie about the gift that they were making to the early church, and it was Peter who confronted them. We read Peter's response to their lie in Acts 5:1–4:

> But a certain man named Ananias, with Sapphira his wife, sold a possession. And he kept back part of the proceeds, his wife also being aware of it, and brought a certain part and laid it at the apostles' feet. But Peter said, "Ananias, why has Satan filled your heart to lie to the Holy Spirit and keep back part of the price of the land for yourself? While it remained, was it not your own? And after it was sold, was it not in your own control? Why have you conceived this thing in your heart? You have not lied to men but to God."

☙ How did Peter function as a prophet in the two passages above?

⮞ What resulted from Peter's prophetic confrontation in number 1 (Acts 2)? What resulted in number 2 (Acts 5)? How did each confrontation influence the body of Christ?

3. The gift of prophecy requires the prophet to be honest about himself and to seek correction for his own error. The genuine prophet of God will always want the truth to reign in his own life, just as he demands truth in the lives of others. It is a false prophet who requires truth in others while not confronting the truth of his own life. Jesus commanded Peter on one occasion to launch into the deep and let down his nets for a catch—which Peter did reluctantly and with doubt. The result, however, was a net-breaking load of fish. Peter recognized his own doubt and failure in this situation and responded as a genuine prophet responds. "He fell down at Jesus' knees saying, 'Depart from me, for I am a sinful man, O Lord'" (Luke 5:8).

4. The gift of prophecy is often voiced as a defense of the church, God's people, God's programs, or God's nature. The genuine prophet is a strong advocate of God's work, although he never takes credit for what God does—to do so would make him party to a lie. The genuine prophet stands up for the veracity of God's Word and the manifestations of God's Spirit. The genuine prophet always points to Jesus as Savior, Deliverer, Healer, and Lord.

Peter and John, on another occasion, spoke to a lame man at the Beautiful Gate of the Temple—and the man was miraculously healed by God. The people around them began to credit Peter and John with the power to heal, but Peter was quick to set the matter in proper order. When Peter saw what was happening, he responded to the people:

> Men of Israel, why do you marvel at this? Or why look so intently at us, as though by our own power or godliness we had made this man walk? The God of Abraham, Isaac, and Jacob, the God of our fathers, glorified His Servant Jesus . . . And His name, through faith in His name, has made this man strong, whom you see and know. Yes, the faith which comes through Him has given him this perfect soundness in the presence of you all.
>
> —Acts 3:12, 13, 16

How might the onlookers have made the mistake of crediting Peter and John with the lame man's healing? Why was he so quick to remedy that misunderstanding?

When have you seen people make a similar mistake? When have you given credit to something or someone other than God?

5. The gift of prophecy functions without regard to personal consequences for the prophet. The genuine prophet sees the consequences of wickedness and is more concerned that those consequences be averted than he is about his own welfare. Peter and John were imprisoned for proclaiming Jesus as the Messiah, and they were told not to teach in the name of Jesus. Here is how Peter responded:

> But Peter and John answered and said to them, "Whether it is right in the sight of God to listen to you more than to God, you judge. For we cannot but speak the things which we have seen and heard."
>
> —Acts 4:19, 20

What motivated Peter to continue preaching the gospel in spite of persecution? What does this motivation reveal about the gift of prophecy?

How is this different from using Scripture as a weapon to browbeat others? How does a person draw a distinction between these two approaches to the gospel?

The Characteristics of a Prophet

As you may have concluded from reading about Peter, the person who has the motivational gift of prophecy will have the following character traits:

- **Boldness:** Prophets are often very bold and direct. They may come across as being fearless or blunt, when in fact they are actually fearful only that God will be displeased with them for any hesitancy in confronting a lie.
- **Simple answers that may seem simplistic:** Prophets tend to see problems in black-and-white terms, and they often "cut to the chase" in the solutions that they offer. They want "bottom-line" facts and are quick to take immediate action.
- **Persuasiveness:** Prophets usually do their utmost to evoke change. They will use whatever means are available to them to argue for the truth.
- **A desire for immediate change:** Prophets have little tolerance for lengthy discussion, group consensus, phased-in changes, or slow processes.
- **Strong dependence on Scripture:** The genuine prophet bases his understanding of truth on the Word of God.
- **Loyalty:** Prophets have a deep and abiding commitment to the truth and to the Lord. This devotion is to the death. Prophets may seem fearless in their commitment.
- **Brokenness:** The genuine prophet has a willingness to be broken by God so that he can be more closely conformed to the likeness of Jesus Christ.
- **Quick judgment and speech:** Prophets often come across as reactionary and impulsive because they see right and wrong clearly and have no tolerance for lies. They are quick to confront lies and errors.

✎ Can you identify someone who demonstrates the gift of prophecy? Do you have this gift?

✎ What tends to be your emotional response to someone who has the gift of prophecy? How can it be misused? Why is it of vital importance to the church when used correctly?

Vital in the Church

Prophets are vital for the church, and they are direct in what they say. They are like a strong spice: they give flavor and identity, as well as direction.

Prophets can be very effective for the gospel when they are operating under the guidance of the Holy Spirit in humility, love, and peace. They can also be destructive when they function "in the flesh" and are not one-hundred-percent reliant upon the Holy Spirit at all times.

We must pray for those who are prophets to be strong and true to God's Word. Above all, we must test their words against the Word of God and heed what they say when they accurately reveal error or deceit in our midst.

Jesus: Our Role Model

Finally, we must recognize that Jesus was a prophet. He is the supreme role model for all prophets to follow. He spoke the truth of God always, regardless of circumstances or consequences, but He always spoke God's truth with love as His motivation and always had the cleansing of human hearts and reconciliation with God the Father as His goal.

> But he who prophesies speaks edification and exhortation and comfort to men.
>
> —1 Corinthians 14:3

☙ Define the following terms, giving practical examples of each:

Edification:

Exhortation:

Comfort:

How does a person exercise the gift of prophecy with the preceding qualifications? What happens when those qualifications are not present?

❧ Today and Tomorrow ❧

TODAY: A PERSON WITH THE GIFT OF PROPHECY WILL HAVE A PASSION FOR TRUTH AND GOD'S WORD.

TOMORROW: I WILL ASK THE LORD TO INCREASE MY ZEAL FOR HIS WORD THIS WEEK, WHETHER OR NOT HE HAS GIVEN ME THE GIFT OF PROPHECY.

LESSON 4

The Gift of Service

┌───┐

❧ In This Lesson ☙

LEARNING: WHAT IS THE GIFT OF SERVICE?

GROWING: HOW IS THIS DIFFERENT FROM JESUS' COMMAND TO HAVE A
SERVANT'S HEART?

└───┘

Are you motivated to pursue practical areas of service to others? Are you concerned with the practical, tangible work associated with a project? Do you enjoy doing things with your hands and in association with other people? You may have the motivational gift of service.

In the Bible, Timothy—the spiritual son and coworker of the apostle Paul—is a man who had the gift of serving. He is an excellent role model for us.

Characteristics of the Gift of Serving

The gift of service has a number of facets to it, among which are the following five characteristics:

1. A person with the gift of service is alert to practical needs and has a desire to meet them. The person with this gift has a heightened sensitivity to those in need and has a compassionate heart that can't help but reach out to meet a need. The servant's greatest satisfaction comes in seeing a need met, in part or in full, through his or her efforts.

The person with a gift of service has a great desire to bring pleasure and joy to others. One manifestation of this desire is usually a great memory concerning the likes and dislikes of other people. People with this gift often go far beyond what is required to meet a need. They truly seek to *bless* others, not simply to provide the bare minimum.

Paul wrote this about Timothy: "But I trust in the Lord Jesus to send Timothy to you shortly, that I also may be encouraged when I know your state. For I have no one like-minded, who will sincerely care for your state" (Philippians 2:19, 20). Paul didn't know anyone who would care for the Philippians with the same tenderness, love, and diligence as Timothy.

Paul was also on the receiving end of Timothy's ministry of service. Notice what he says to Timothy in 2 Timothy 4:9–13:

> Be diligent to come to me quickly . . . Get Mark and bring him with you, for he is useful to me for ministry . . . Bring the cloak that I left with Carpus at Troas when you come—and the books, especially the parchments.

Paul knew that he could trust Timothy with these very practical concerns because Timothy was gifted to serve in this way. We also find in Acts 19:20 that Timothy was one of two people who ministered to Paul. Timothy cared for Paul's practical needs and assisted him in every way possible.

☙ Do you know someone who has the gift of service? Do you have this gift?

~ How is the *gift* of service different from the *ministry* of being a servant? In what ways are all Christians called to be servants? How is the gifted person's ministry likely to be unique?

2. The person with a gift of serving has joy when he knows that the service frees another person to engage more fully in the ministry to which he has been called. Those with a gift of service delight in preparing the background details and doing the backstage work that allows others to perform to the best of their abilities, because they take joy in the accomplishments and success of others. They often are dismayed when they see the person whom they are serving squandering time or devoting energy to things that are unproductive. On the other hand, if they see the person whom they are serving focusing energy and doing the work to which God has called him or her, they have great delight and a deep feeling of satisfaction.

The person with this gift is very generous in giving time, energy, and effort, and especially so if worthwhile projects are undertaken and completed as a result. At times, others may mistake the motives of the person with a gift of service because the person is always eager to undertake another project or tackle another need.

~ How do you feel when you are a part of a team doing work unto the Lord with diligence and faithfulness?

How do you react when your service goes unnoticed or unappreciated? Do you tend to become discouraged, or do you simply look for another opportunity to serve?

3. The person with the gift of service tends to ignore his own needs and to overextend personal energy and strength. Those with this gift are often so concerned with getting a job done that they overlook the passing of time or the meeting of their personal needs, including health. A mother with this gift of service will often work untiringly long into the night to meet the needs of her family, even to the neglect of her own physical needs.

Paul wrote to Timothy, "No longer drink only water, but use a little wine for your stomach's sake and your frequent infirmities" (1 Tim. 5:23). Paul sent Timothy to some very difficult places to minister. For example, he sent him to Crete—one of the most difficult places to preach the gospel and nurture a group of new believers. In writing to Titus, Paul quoted a Cretan who said about his own people, "Cretans are always liars, evil beasts, lazy gluttons." Paul added, "This testimony is true" (Titus 1:12, 13). Timothy no doubt encountered numerous stressful and difficult situations and people in the course of his ministry on the island of Crete, and yet he was so faithful in his service that he neglected his own health.

The downside for the person with the gift of service is that he may be so highly motivated to help another person that he overlooks the emotional needs of his own family. He may get so wrapped up in meeting the needs of those he sees as genuinely "needy" that he neglects the less obvious and more basic needs of those closest to him.

I charge you before God and the Lord Jesus Christ and the elect angels that you observe these things without prejudice, doing nothing with partiality. Do not lay hands on anyone hastily, nor share in other people's sins; keep yourself pure. No longer drink only water, but use a little wine for your stomach's sake and your frequent infirmities.

—1 Timothy 5:21–23

⮞ Notice that Paul's admonition to Timothy concerning his health is in the context of a command, not a recommendation. Why was it necessary for Paul to make such a command?

⮞ How might it be tempting for a person with the gift of service to think that ignoring personal or family needs is commendable? In what ways might it actually be a misuse of that gift?

4. The person with the gift of serving has a need to be appreciated for his service to confirm that it is necessary, valued, and beneficial. People with this gift have no desire to waste their time or efforts on things that will be of little benefit. They are so concerned with the overall success of a project or ministry that they do not want to waste any of their own energies on things that will be of little consequence.

People with this gift are motivated when others appreciate their service because it confirms for them that their ministry is productive and not wasted. They will want to do even more for the person who acknowledges and is thankful for their contribution. As you work with others who have this gift of service, ask yourself, "How can I show my appreciation to this person who is giving so much of his time, talent, and energy?" Paul was quick to praise Timothy and to acknowledge his efforts. He wrote to the Corinthians:

> And if Timothy comes, see that he may be with you without fear; for he does the work of the Lord, as I also do. Therefore let no one despise him.

> —1 Corinthians 16:10, 11

Why does a person with the gift of service need to hear positive affirmation? How is this different from desiring the praise of others?

What godly servants do you know? How can you serve them in return with a spirit of gratitude this week?

5. The person with a gift of serving has a strong desire to be with other people. Those with this gift are not loners, they are "people persons." They enjoy being with people because the more people they meet, the more opportunities they have to discover and respond to needs in the lives of others.

In Acts 19–20, we find Timothy mentioned several times. Each time he is mentioned with someone else. In Acts 19:22, he is mentioned with Erastus; and in Acts 20:4, Timothy is part of a team that is working with Paul, including Sopater, Aristarchus, Secundus, Gaius, Tychicus, and Trophimus. People with the gift of service find their greatest sense of fulfillment in being with people and relating to them in practical ways.

The person with a gift of service doesn't need his name in headlines. He doesn't need to be in the spotlight—but he does need to be in relationship with other people.

When you work on a project, do you prefer to do it all yourself or to enlist the help of others?

When someone else asks for your help on a project, do you tend to take the leadership or do you tend to look for background tasks?

6. Those with the gift of service feel that they must respond to the practical needs they see. They quickly perceive needs and are compelled to act. They must act. They cannot sit still in the face of a need.

At times, the person with a gift of service may seem pushy because he is willing to volunteer and to get started with a task. They almost have the attitude, "If you just get out of my way and cut all the red tape, I'll get this done for you in no time." They have little tolerance for rules and procedures seen as unnecessary for the completion of a task.

7. Those with the gift of service are most effective in working on short-range projects. They gravitate naturally toward projects that can be completed in relatively short periods of time. People with the gift of serving tend to be frustrated by long-range projects; they need immediate signs of progress to validate the effort and time they are giving. If a project is going to take five years, it should be turned over to a person who has the gift of leadership or administration; then that person should recruit those with the gift of service who can take smaller pieces of that project and see them to completion.

☙ Do you gravitate toward short-term or long-term projects? Do you have long-range vision, or do you tend to notice other service projects that can be immediately fulfilled?

8. Those with the gift of service often feel very unqualified and inadequate for ministry. They often do not perceive that they are ministers; they simply see themselves as practical, can-do people. Paul encouraged Timothy in this way on one occasion: "This charge I commit to you, son Timothy, according to the prophecies previously made concerning you, that by them you may wage the good warfare, having faith and a good conscience" (1 Tim. 1:18, 19).

Timothy may very well have been discouraged into thinking that he was unqualified for the task that Paul had given him. Paul reminds him of prophecies which confirm that Timothy is doing what God desires him to do, and that he has what it takes to engage in successful spiritual warfare.

Five Things to Guard Against

The person with the gift of serving has to be especially sensitive to the following potentially negative aspects of service.

1. The person with the gift of serving must guard against becoming discouraged if others fail to appreciate his service. Service should always be undertaken as unto the Lord. People will disappoint us in their lack of appreciation and will fail to acknowledge acts of service, but God sees all of our acts of service, and He is a faithful rewarder of those who serve with diligence and faithfulness.

2. The person with the gift of serving must guard against doing so much for others that he never gives others an opportunity to give in return. My own mother had a great gift of service. She was so good at anticipating needs in others that very often she was halfway finished meeting a need before I had an opportunity to voice the need! Many gifted servants actually feel guilty if they allow others to serve them; yet, ironically, allowing others to serve you can be an act of service in itself. Learn to receive from others. If you fail to do so, you will be robbing others of the rewards that come from giving.

☙ When have you been frustrated by not being allowed to serve another person? How might you have been blessed if your service had been accepted?

3. **The person with the gift of serving must be sensitive to what God is attempting to teach another person.** At times, we can be too quick to meet the needs in the lives of others—to the point where we negate the lesson that God is attempting to convey to them.

4. **The person with the gift of serving must remain attentive to personal spiritual growth and to the disciplines of prayer, praise, and the reading of Scripture.** He must fight the tendency to be so busy with practical tasks that spiritual growth suffers. Martha was a friend of Jesus and sister to Lazarus and Mary, and she was very concerned about serving. Jesus recognized the value of her gift and her service, but encouraged her in saying, "Martha, Martha, you are worried and troubled about many things. But one thing is needed, and Mary has chosen that good part, which will not be taken away from her" (Luke 10:41, 42). Jesus called Martha to a time of relaxing in His presence, listening to Him and enjoying His fellowship.

🔊 What did Jesus mean by "that good part" which Mary had chosen? How had Martha's gift of service actually worked against her at that point?

5. **The person with this gift must avoid the tendency to get sidetracked by more urgent needs—to the point where the original need may not be met.** People with the gift of service are quick to notice the needs of others around them, but there can be times when there are more needs than one person can hope to meet. Sometimes discretion is needed to determine which needs are top priorities, focusing on those which are important and ignoring those which are merely urgent.

Hallmarks of Godly Service

The Bible admonishes us in a number of ways about how to engage in godly service one to another. We are to serve in this way:

~ **Be alert:** Ask the Holy Spirit to show you precisely what needs you are to meet and how best to meet them.

~ **Be hospitable:** Show kindness and consideration to others as you serve them. Be gracious to others in the way that you speak to them and assist them.

~ **Be generous:** Give generously, but be aware that you are not responsible for meeting all the needs of another person—indeed, you are incapable of being the sole source of answers or provision for another person. Only God can meet all the needs in a person's life.

~ **Be joyful:** Do your service with a joyful heart. Inspire others to praise and give thanks to God.

~ **Be flexible:** Should the Lord reveal to you a different way of serving or an unusual avenue for service that you have not pursued before, be willing to obey Him explicitly.

~ **Be available:** Do not hide behind false humility if you are asked to minister in a way that seems a challenge to you. Virtually every type of ministry needs those who are willing and gifted to serve.

~ **Be diligent in seeing a project to its completion:** Don't allow yourself to become sidetracked or to spread yourself too thin.

And whatever you do, do it heartily, as to the Lord and not to men, knowing that from the Lord you will receive the reward of the inheritance; for you serve the Lord Christ.

—Colossians 3:23, 24

39

✎ In practical terms, what does it mean to perform a service "as to the Lord"? What does it mean to perform it "to men"?

✎ How does an act of service serve Jesus? Why is this distinction vitally important to those who have the gift of service?

Jesus—The Greatest Servant of All

One of the names given to Jesus was that of Servant. He taught His disciples:

> For I have given you an example, that you should do as I have done to you. Most assuredly, I say to you, a servant is not greater than his master; nor is he who is sent greater than he who sent him. If you know these things, blessed are you if you do them.
>
> —John 13:15–17

Jesus said this to His disciples after He had washed their feet—a lowly task usually done by household servants. As Jesus humbled Himself to serve, so we must humble ourselves to serve. No act of service to another human being should ever be considered too lowly or beneath our dignity.

In employing our gift of service, we must always keep Jesus as our role model. We are to serve in His name, for His glory, and in the same manner of love that He showed to others. Jesus served with a sacrificial heart. He gave His all. He calls those who are given the gift of service to do the same.

What did Jesus mean when He said, "A servant is not greater than his master"? In what ways might we consider ourselves better than Jesus when it comes to serving others?

What types of service do you consider beneath your dignity? When has someone performed such a service for you?

Today and Tomorrow

TODAY: ALL CHRISTIANS ARE CALLED TO BE SERVANTS, BUT SOME HAVE A SPECIAL GIFT OF SERVING OTHERS.

TOMORROW: I WILL ASK THE LORD TO TEACH ME HOW TO SERVE OTHERS LIKE HIM, WHETHER OR NOT I HAVE THE GIFT OF SERVICE.

LESSON 5

The Gift of Teaching

───────── ❧ **In This Lesson** ❧ ─────────

LEARNING: HOW CAN I KNOW IF I HAVE THE GIFT OF TEACHING?

GROWING: WHAT ARE THE MOST IMPORTANT ASPECTS OF BEING A TEACHER?

───────── ∞ ─────────

Are you concerned with accuracy when the Word of God is taught? Are you concerned that the truth is passed on to the next generation or to those who currently are lacking in understanding and wisdom? Do you desire to see the lives of others changed as a result of information being given to them? You may have the motivational gift of teaching.

Those with other gifts may be teachers, but their motivation for teaching is not the pursuit of God's truth. A person may become a Sunday school teacher out of love and compassion for children. That person is motivated to teach by a gift of mercy. Another person may be motivated to teach because he is concerned that too much emphasis is being placed upon the application of Scripture and not enough on the black-and-white, right-and-wrong absolutes of the Bible. That person is motivated to teach out of a ministry gift of prophecy. The person who is gifted to teach is motivated solely because he loves the truth and wants to impart God's Word with accuracy and clarity to others.

One of the foremost teachers in the Bible is Luke. Just look at how he begins his gospel account:

Inasmuch as many have taken in hand to set in order a narra-
tive of those things which have been fulfilled among us, just
as those who from the beginning were eyewitnesses and ministers of the word delivered them to us, it seemed good to me
also, having had perfect understanding of all things from the
very first, to write to you an orderly account, most excellent
Theophilus, that you may know the certainty of those things in
which you were instructed.

—Luke 1:1–4

Luke says of himself that he is an expert, that his understanding is
"perfect," and that his account will be orderly. His desire is that Theophilus might "know with certainty," that he might know with exact-
ness of detail. Luke's Gospel and the book of Acts are highly detailed
accounts that are intended to teach the truth with certainty that Jesus
still is the Christ.

⚘ Who are the best teachers that you have learned from? What
made their teaching so effective?

⚘ Do you believe you might have the gift of teaching? Have
other people told you that you do?

Characteristics of the Gift of Teaching

Teaching was considered a highly valued profession in both Jewish and Greek circles. To be a teacher within the early church was an exalted position, and few were called teachers. A great responsibility was placed upon teachers to be accurate, wise, diligent in their research, and skilled in their ability to present information. Then as now, the gift of teaching was expected to display the following seven characteristics:

1. The gift of teaching includes a great concern to provide a systematic sequence. Teachers present material in a way that is easy for others to follow. Luke notes that he is going to write an orderly "account." Another translation of those words would be "consecutive order." The teacher lays out his material so that it all points toward specific themes which convey the main point.

2. The gift of teaching includes a concern with the accuracy of words and the use of language. A teacher is concerned with precise definitions and shades of meaning. A teacher can be irritating at times because he is always asking, "What do you mean by that?" He wants to hear and speak with accuracy.

3. The gift of teaching includes a delight in researching and reporting as many details as possible. The Gospel of Luke contains more details about key events than any other Gospel. Luke sees meaning in details. The person gifted in teaching delights in his own study of Scripture or in his own research. He takes great joy in seeing meaning in factual details that may have been overlooked by others. Once this information has been acquired, the teacher longs to share everything that he knows. At times, that can be more information than others want or need to hear, but the teacher feels compelled to "teach all."

No other Gospel writer tells us about the birth of Jesus as Luke tells us. Nearly three chapters of his Gospel are devoted to the birth of Jesus— he tells the story of Mary and Joseph, and also the stories of Zacharias and Elizabeth, and Simeon and Anna. He deals with the facts of the story, but also with dialogue, monologue, and references to the Old Testament.

> [Christ] we preach, warning every man and teaching every man in all wisdom, that we may present every man perfect in Christ Jesus.
>
> —Colossians 1:28

∽ What does it mean to "present every man perfect in Christ Jesus"? How is this done?

∽ What is the role of the teacher in the above process? What is the role of the teacher's audience?

4. The gift of teaching includes a great interest in knowing as much as possible about a subject being studied. A teacher never tires of delving into a chosen area of study, or engaging in multiple studies with increasing depth over time. The teacher wants all of the information which he presents to be accurate, valid, and verifiable. Traditional historical accounts tell us that Luke took several years to research his Gospel, talking to numerous people who had known Jesus personally.

5. The gift of teaching is concerned with the acquisition of knowledge and understanding, both of which are vital to wisdom. The prophet is concerned that a person makes the right decision and recognizes fully what is at stake if the wrong decision is made. A changed life is the goal. The person who exhorts is concerned that others understand the step-by-step process necessary to reach a particular goal and admonishes them that no step should be omitted or overlooked. A correction is the goal. The teacher, by comparison, is concerned that others know the Bible and the commandments of God with precision and full understanding. Acquisition of knowledge is the goal, as Luke wrote to Theophilus, "that you may know the certainty of those things in which you were instructed" (Luke1:4).

6. The gift of teaching is primarily concerned with fact, not illustration or application. Teachers are rarely impulsive and often reject emotional material or illustrations. They nearly always have a tendency toward logic and organization. They are not likely to delight in lengthy discussion. In fact, they can quickly become irritated with those who talk too much, and especially so if the person doesn't seem to know what he is talking about!

7. The gift of teaching is usually pursued in a very systematic way. Most teachers have developed a personal method for doing research and presenting information to others. They develop a means for determining what is true. They sift all things necessary for their method before drawing a conclusion.

Let the word of Christ dwell in you richly in all wisdom, teaching and admonishing one another in psalms and hymns and
spiritual songs, singing with grace in your hearts to the Lord.

—Colossians 3:16

❧ What does it mean to "let the word of Christ dwell in you
richly"? How is this done? What role does wisdom play in the
process?

❧ What does it mean to "admonish" someone? How is this different from teaching? How do the two work together?

Words of Caution for the Teacher

The goal of a teacher within the Body of Christ must be to present Jesus
Christ to others, with the intent that others grow up in their faith to be
more like Jesus. The purpose is not to convince others of the teacher's
own intellect or degree of information, but rather to convince others to
accept Jesus Christ and become more mature in their Christian lives.

A teacher must be a good communicator. Too often, teachers are content to present the facts as they have studied them, without making their subject matter of interest or application to their students. For true learning to occur, one must be a good researcher and organizer of information—and also an effective communicator, a person who knows how to convey information in a way that will captivate the will and attention of those who hear him speak or read his writing.

A teacher must be open to new means of presenting information. Teachers have a tendency to be too narrow in their interpretation of what is information, fact, or knowledge. They see straightforward declarative statements as more desirable than telling stories, even though stories are an excellent vehicle for conveying the truth of God's Word. Jesus, of course, was a master at telling parables, the use of stories to convey spiritual truth. Most teachers can benefit from incorporating more illustrations and applications into their factual presentations.

A teacher must not get hung up on small errors in detail. Too often, teachers dismiss an entire presentation solely on the basis of one particular error. They need to be able to sift error from truth.

A teacher must always be open to the intuitive spiritual leading of the Holy Spirit to discern truth. Truth is more than facts. Many teachers rely mostly on their own intellectual abilities and skills to evaluate situations. They must also be open to hearing what the Holy Spirit may whisper into their hearts and minds.

A teacher must always look for the big picture. Some teachers become too narrow in their approach and fail to see the broad background or the general direction. We must be open at all times to have an enlarged vision of what the Lord wants to do in our world today and what role He desires for us.

A teacher must never substitute academic degrees for genuine wisdom from God. I have met numerous people who have had very little formal education but who have had a great understanding of both God's Word and the ways in which God works in the human heart. I have also met people who have had a string of degrees behind their names who could barely communicate with sense and who had no understanding of God. Formal education is not a qualifier for the gift of teaching. We must never look down on those who have this genuine motivational gift without formal degrees—and neither must we exalt those who call themselves teachers solely because they have completed degrees but have no gift of God for teaching.

> Be diligent to present yourself approved to God, a worker who does not need to be ashamed, rightly dividing the word of truth.
>
> —2 Timothy 2:15

What does it mean to be "rightly dividing the word of truth"? How is this done? What steps are involved?

What does it mean to be "a worker who does not need to be ashamed"? Of what might a teacher be ashamed before God? How is this avoided?

Qualities of the Godly Teacher

Those who have been gifted as teachers are challenged by the Word of God to exhibit these behaviors:

∽ **Self-control:** an ability to focus on the issue at hand and to avoid all detours as they prepare the lesson that they are to teach.

∽ **Reverence and respect for the Word of God:** seeking the truth of God's Word, never approaching it with the intent of disputing it or denying its validity.

∽ **Diligence and thoroughness:** sticking to the study and research until they have a thorough knowledge of the subject and have prepared diligently the best lesson possible.

∽ **Dependability:** so that others can always rely upon them to "rightly divide" the Word of truth.

Those who operate under the guidance of the Holy Spirit and who recognize that they are gifted as teachers will not find teaching to be a burden—rather, these behaviors will be the natural way that they respond to any opportunity to teach. To the person gifted in teaching, there is no greater joy than to study the Bible and then share what has been learned.

How can a young man cleanse his way? By taking heed according to Your word. With my whole heart I have sought You; oh, let me not wander from Your commandments! Your word I have hidden in my heart, that I might not sin against You.

—Psalm 119:9–11

50

❧ According to these verses, what is required of a person who wants to teach others from God's Word?

❧ What role does verbal communication play in teaching others? What role does one's example play? How do the above verses apply to each?

Being Aware of False Teachers

Jesus made a very clear statement about teaching in Matthew 5:19:

> Whoever therefore breaks one of the least of these commandments, and teaches men so, shall be called least in the kingdom of heaven; but whoever does and teaches them, he shall be called great in the kingdom of heaven.

A teacher's first obligation is always to make sure that he personally lives by the truth. It is a false teacher who says one thing and then lives another. Teachers must recognize that they always teach, not only with their words but by the example of their lives. Repeatedly in Scripture, we find admonitions to be aware of false teachers who come into the church. As you read through the verses on the following page, note especially the behaviors of false teachers.

But there were also false prophets among the people, even as there will be false teachers among you, who will secretly bring in destructive heresies, even denying the Lord who bought them, and bring on themselves swift destruction. And many will follow their destructive ways, because of whom the way of truth will be blasphemed. By covetousness they will exploit you with deceptive words; for a long time their judgment has not been idle, and their destruction does not slumber.

—2 Peter 2:1–3

➣ What tactics do false teachers use to deceive people, according to these verses? How does the process work? How can one identify a false teacher?

➣ What "destructive heresies" are being taught in the church today? How are people being led astray by false teachers?

Jesus was the Master Teacher

The disciples of Jesus frequently addressed Him as "Teacher." Jesus taught by example, by illustration, and by direct presentation of information. He was a consummate teacher in every way. Matthew describes Jesus' ministry as one of teaching, preaching, and healing—and in each instance, teaching is the first aspect of His ministry that is mentioned. (See Matthew 4:23 as an example.) Consider Jesus' Sermon on the Mount (Matt. 5–7) and note the way that this sermon is prefaced: "And seeing the multitudes, He went up on a mountain, and when He was seated His disciples came to Him. Then He opened His mouth and *taught* them" (Matt. 5:1, 2, italics added). Jesus made teaching a part of His great commission to His disciples, saying, "Go therefore and make disciples of all nations . . . teaching them to observe all things that I have commanded you" (Matt. 28:19, 20). I encourage you to read through the Sermon on the Mount and note the many ways in which Jesus embodied and demonstrated good teaching.

∼ Read through Matthew 5–7, taking note of Jesus' teaching methods. Notice how He uses:

Facts:

Stories:

Metaphors:

Personal examples:

❧ What practical application can Jesus' example from these chapters have for someone with the gift of teaching?

❧ Today and Tomorrow ❧

TODAY: A TEACHER TEACHES AS MUCH BY EXAMPLE AS BY WORD.

TOMORROW: I WILL DILIGENTLY EXAMINE MY OWN LIFE THIS WEEK, LOOK-
ING FOR AREAS WHERE MY ACTIONS DON'T MATCH THE TEACH-
INGS OF THE WORD OF GOD.

LESSON 6

The Gift of Exhortation

━━━━━━━━ ❧ **In This Lesson** ☙ ━━━━━━━━

LEARNING: WHAT EXACTLY IS EXHORTATION?

GROWING: HOW DOES ONE USE A GIFT OF EXHORTATION IN DAILY LIFE?

❧

Are you vitally concerned about correcting error wherever and whenever you find it? Do you care deeply about helping others to avoid mistakes, and helping those who have made mistakes to repent of their ways and return to righteousness before God? You may have the motivational gift of exhortation. One of the key biblical figures who exemplifies the gift of exhortation is the apostle Paul. Here is the heart of Paul's motivation for ministry:

> Him we preach, warning every man and teaching every man in all wisdom, that we may present every man perfect in Christ Jesus. To this end I also labor, striving according to His working which works in me mightily.

> —Colossians 1:28, 29

The word *warning* in this passage has also been translated as "admonishing" or "exhorting." Exhortation always has an element of caution and concern about it: the exhorter desires to see every believer stay on the straight and narrow path that leads to both heavenly and earthly rewards.

⟋ What does the word "exhort" mean, in your own words? Give practical, real-life examples of exhortation.

⟋ Do you know someone who has been given the gift of exhortation? Have you been given this motivational gift?

Before you become alarmed and think that you might be called to all of the perils and suffering that Paul endured, let me assure you of two things. First, many are called to exhortation, but not all are called to be apostles. Those who have a gift of exhortation may have a quiet and retiring spirit—but on occasion, they speak with a certainty and finality in their tone that lets everyone around them know that what they say is true and should be heeded. Second, many are called to exhortation in the church, but not all are called to exhort groups of people. Exhortation often is given in a one-on-one setting. Central to the gift of the exhortation is a heart that desires to encourage other Christians and to see them become all that they can be in Christ Jesus.

Jesus described the work of the Holy Spirit this way: "I tell you the truth. It is to your advantage that I go away; for if I do not go away, the Helper will not come to you; but if I depart, I will send Him to you" (John 16:7). The word translated "Helper" in this verse is the Greek word *Parakletos*, the same word used for *exhorter*. The person with a gift of exhortation is called alongside another believer to help that person understand and adhere to the truth. The person who is a genuine *helper* or *exhorter* encourages others by presence, word, and deed to continue forward in following Jesus Christ.

Jesus: A Portrait of Exhortation

As with all the motivational gifts, Jesus is our role model in the gift of exhortation. Think about the way that Jesus dealt with people in need. He was not a negative person. He never shamed people or belittled them. The only people that He did not encourage were the Pharisees and Sadducees because they put great burdens of guilt and shame on others.

Recall specifically how Jesus dealt with a woman who was caught in the act of adultery. Jesus said to the men who accused her, "He who is without sin among you, let him throw a stone at her first" (John 8:7). When all of her accusers went away, "being convicted by their conscience" (v. 9), Jesus was left alone with the woman. "He said to her, 'Woman, where are those accusers of yours? Has no one condemned you?' She said, 'No one, Lord.' And Jesus said to her, 'Neither do I condemn you; go and sin no more'" (John 8:10, 11).

Neither do I condemn you. Go and sin no more. That is the spirit and those are the hallmark words of the person who exhorts. Forgiveness, admonition not to sin, compassion, an awareness of a person's potential in Jesus Christ—each of these is to be manifested in exhortation and should be at the core of what an exhorter says and does.

The exhorter should be quick to say, "I accept you, I love you in Jesus Christ. I believe in who God created you to be and who He is calling you to be as His beloved child. I recognize that you have sinned, but I forgive you. Now, go and sin no more."

꼭. Why did Jesus forgive the woman caught in adultery in John 8? What were her accusers hoping Jesus would do?

꼭. How did Jesus' response to her demonstrate the gift of exhortation? How does an exhorter respond when confronted with sinful behavior?

Characteristics of the Gift of Exhortation

The gift of exhortation is characterized by the following eight principles.

1. The person with a gift of exhortation desires to see others mature in their faith. The exhorter desires to see that others are growing in their spiritual lives. Exhorters are people oriented, discipleship oriented, growth oriented, and maturity oriented. Read again what Paul said to the Colossians: "warning every man . . . that we may present every man perfect in Jesus Christ" (Col. 1:28). The exhorter is quick to ask, "Where are you in your spiritual life? Are you growing? In what ways?"

2. The person with a gift of exhortation desires to see others discover their spiritual potential. The exhorter does not want another person to be anything less than what God has called him to be. The person with this gift usually can discern the potential of another person and can visualize his spiritual achievement. The exhorter has insight as to what God might do in and through a person if that person yielded all of his talents, abilities, and energy to the Lord. Once an exhorter sees your potential, he feels compelled to encourage you to reach your potential and to turn away from anything that might diminish your growth in Christ.

> And when they had preached the gospel to that city and made many disciples, they returned to Lystra, Iconium, and Antioch, strengthening the souls of the disciples, exhorting them to continue in the faith, and saying, "We must through many tribulations enter the kingdom of God."

> —Acts 14:21, 22

❧ What does it mean that we must enter the kingdom of God "through many tribulations"? What role do tribulations play in a Christian's growth?

❧ In what way did it strengthen the souls of the disciples to be warned about such tribulations? How does such a warning fit in with the gift of exhortation?

3. The person with a gift of exhortation is quick to ask about the spiritual welfare of others. The exhorter will do his utmost to find a way of communicating with another person. The exhorter is "other oriented"—he will ask questions and probe until he is satisfied that the person is growing in Jesus Christ. If he discovers an error or blockage in another's growth, he will be quick to point it out and will identify the steps that need to be taken for the person to get back on track with the Lord. Paul never hesitated to say to others, "I have heard this about you," and then he always went on to give God's wisdom for how the problem should be resolved.

The exhorter may seem to be too aggressive or too personal in the eyes of someone who is choosing sin or who is apathetic toward growing spiritually. The person who comes face to face with exhortation may feel as if he is on the hot seat. The exhorter, however, is not trying to produce guilt or shame, if he is truly following the leading of the Holy Spirit. Rather, he wants to help the other person move forward in a personal relationship with the Lord. A number of people with this gift gravitate toward a career in counseling because they want to see others grow, develop, and become sound in their faith.

4. The godly exhorter must always point others toward Jesus Christ. The truth of God's Word and the message of God's salvation through Christ must always be central to exhortation. Otherwise, the exhorter is only giving human advice and human wisdom. To be operating with the spiritual gift of exhortation, the exhorter must identify ways in which a person can turn to Christ and to the Holy Spirit, following Jesus Christ as his example and trusting in the Holy Spirit for daily guidance. (This is true, of course, for any person who wants to be an effective witness for Jesus Christ.) Paul's entire theme for the churches was this: "Christ Jesus in me, and I in Christ Jesus."

Therefore humble yourselves under the mighty hand of God, that He may exalt you in due time, casting all your care upon Him, for He cares for you. Be sober, be vigilant; because your adversary the devil walks about like a roaring lion, seeking whom he may devour. Resist him, steadfast in the faith, knowing that the same sufferings are experienced by your brotherhood in the world. . . I have written to you briefly, exhorting and testifying that this is the true grace of God in which you stand.

—1 Peter 5:6–9, 12

᠅ What elements of exhortation are demonstrated in the verses above?

᠅ How can Paul's exhortation in these verses help you to exhort others? To be exhorted yourself?

5. The gift of exhortation includes the ability to give precise instructions about how a person might grow in relationship with Christ. Those with this gift have an ability to understand precisely what is necessary for people to make corrections in their lives and move forward without hindrances. Exhorters are "step one, step two, step three" people; they understand the steps necessary for people to apply the truth of God's Word to their lives. Throughout his letters, Paul writes step-by-step instructions for the believers to mature in their faith. His arguments for the faith are well organized and completely thought through so that those who read his admonitions understand clearly what he is saying and desiring on their behalf.

6. The person with the gift of exhortation has learned value in suffering. The exhorter desires to see a person avoid suffering and to come through hardship victoriously, but the godly exhorter also has learned that suffering can have great value in a person's life in breaking old patterns of sin and adopting new patterns of right behavior. Paul learned the lessons associated with suffering. He wrote to the Corinthians,

> And He said to me, "My grace is sufficient for you, for My strength is made perfect in weakness." Therefore most gladly I will rather boast in my infirmities, that the power of Christ may rest upon me. Therefore I take pleasure in infirmities, in reproaches, in needs, in persecutions, in distresses, for Christ's sake. For when I am weak, then I am strong.
>
> —2 Corinthians 12:9, 10

The person who exhorts may not appear to be very sympathetic with the person who is suffering, because the exhorter is concerned with helping him take the steps to grow and to make changes to get out of repetitive struggling and suffering. The person who exhorts must exhort with compassion.

〜 When have you seen Christ's power resting on a person who was weak or infirm? How might God's power have been less apparent if the person had not been suffering?

〜 Explain in your own words Paul's paradox: "For when I am weak, then I am strong." How is this possible? How does it work out in real-life, practical terms?

7. The person with the gift of exhortation is concerned with the application of God's Word. The prophet wants to make sure that the truth is proclaimed; the teacher wants to make sure that it is the whole truth and nothing but the truth that is taught. The exhorter asks, "How can this be applied to life? What should a person do with this truth?" Paul is always concerned with how a person is to follow Christ and what a person must do to manifest godly behavior and grow in faith.

The teacher begins with the Word of God and then presents it as opportunities arise. The exhorter looks at the needs of people, then to the Word of God for answers, returning to people with the application of God's Word for them.

8. Those with a gift of exhortation want to be with people and see first-hand how they are growing in their faith. Exhorters are usually very good at reading body language and facial expressions. Paul wrote again and again to the churches, "I long to be with you," "I can hardly wait to see you again," "I was so grateful to hear about you from someone who recently was with you."

One of the chief concerns of those who exhort is to resolve conflicts among groups of people. The person with a gift of exhortation does not shy away from relational problems, but gets right in the middle to help sort them out and bring healing and reconciliation. Paul's writing often focuses on how people should relate to one another, including husbands and wives, parents and children, slaves and slave owners, Jews and Greeks, "bonded" and "free." Paul is always concerned with establishing unity in the Body of Christ.

The person with this gift delights in being around people who are interested in deepening their spiritual lives. He often has little patience with those who want only to live superficially.

> Now I myself am confident concerning you, my brethren, that you also are full of goodness, filled with all knowledge, able also to admonish one another.
>
> —Romans 15:14

What are the prerequisites for being an exhorter, according to this verse? How are these things attained?

☙ In what ways is this verse an exhortation to Paul's audience? How might this exhortation lead others to admonish and exhort one another?

Words of Caution to Those Who Exhort

The person with the gift of exhortation must be cautious in the following areas.

The exhorter must not oversimplify a problem. He must not promise solutions too quickly or give a quick-fix formula. If he does, the person with the need is likely to reject the wisdom as too simplistic. This is not to say that the solution offered is wrong. Rather, the exhorter must deal with others in compassion and lead the person in need through the steps required, one by one.

The exhorter must be able to empathize. He must identify as fully as possible with the person in need. He must try to feel what they feel and see what they see, viewing the world through their eyes in order to understand how to help them see the truth with greater clarity.

The exhorter must not lose sight of the importance of leading people to Jesus Christ. Exhorters are primarily concerned with the growth and maturity of those who are believers, and as such they may be perceived as unconcerned about the lost. Exhorters can be excellent evangelists and witnesses for Christ if they will see their ministries in broader terms of leading people from darkness to light.

The exhorter must be skilled in applying the Word of God within the context of Scripture as a whole. At times, those who exhort are so quick to apply Scripture that they may be tempted to lift a single verse out of context and offer it as a solution. The Bible is as applicable to our lives today as it was to those for whom it was first written, and the exhorter must look for meaning and application that spans all cultures and all history. He must see the entire scope of God's truth.

What is true for an exhorter, of course, is true for all Christians. We must all become skilled in applying the *whole* of God's Word to our lives, in winning others to Christ, and in leading people from where they are to where God wants them to be. The exhorter is one who is gifted in a special way by the Holy Spirit to do this intuitively and responsively.

> Beware, brethren, lest there be in any of you an evil heart of unbelief in departing from the living God; but exhort one another daily, while it is called "Today," lest any of you be hardened through the deceitfulness of sin.
>
> —Hebrews 3:12, 13

How does exhortation help prevent a person from becoming hardened in sin? How does exhortation help to undeceive people?

What does it mean to depart from the living God? How does such a thing happen? What role does exhortation play in avoiding it?

Many Exhorters in the Church

The church needs people who will exhort and encourage others to reach their full potential in Christ. Each of us needs to have at least one person who functions as an exhorter in his or her life. This is a person who asks periodically and sincerely, "What is God doing in your life? What are you doing to develop your relationship with the Lord? In what ways is the Lord working in your life to make you more like Jesus Christ?" An exhorter must be a person who will exemplify this behavior:

Wisdom: to understand the Word of God and how it might be applied to you.

Discernment: to be able to see clearly your spirit and your potential.

Faith: to believe that God can take you from where you are to where He desires you to be.

Discretion: to keep what he knows about you in confidence and to lead you step by step into the greater future that God has for you.

Love: to desire the best in your life and always be willing to give you his best, offering you God's truth without personal judgment or condemnation.

67

 ⌒ **Creative:** to recognize that you are a unique individual, and to help you apply God's Word to your life at any particular moment and in light of particular circumstances.

 ⌒ **Enthusiasm:** to be able to inspire you to desire more in your Christian walk.

If you allow a person with these qualities to help you as he or she receives guidance from the Holy Spirit, you will be greatly blessed! Ask the Lord Jesus to lead you to such a person.

For our exhortation did not come from error or uncleanness, nor was it in deceit. But as we have been approved by God to be entrusted with the gospel, even so we speak, not as pleasing men, but God who tests our hearts. For neither at any time did we use flattering words, as you know, nor a cloak for covetousness—God is witness. Nor did we seek glory from men, either from you or from others, when we might have made demands as apostles of Christ. But we were gentle among you, just as a nursing mother cherishes her own children. So, affectionately longing for you, we were well pleased to impart to you not only the gospel of God, but also our own lives, because you had become dear to us.

—1 Thessalonians 2:3–8

 ⌒ List the qualities of an exhorter which are illustrated by this passage.

List the things that are *not* qualities of an exhorter, as illustrated by this passage.

☙ Today and Tomorrow ❧

TODAY: AN EXHORTER SPURS OTHERS ON TO BECOME MORE LIKE CHRIST.

TOMORROW: I WILL CONSCIOUSLY STRIVE TO BECOME MORE LIKE CHRIST MYSELF IN THE COMING WEEK.

The Gift of Giving

—— ❧ **In This Lesson** ❧ ——

LEARNING: HOW IS THE GIFT OF GIVING DIFFERENT FROM REGULAR TITHING?

GROWING: WHAT ROLE DOES A GIVER PLAY IN THE BODY OF CHRIST?

Do you respond immediately to the presence of a need by saying, "What can I do? How can I help solve this need?" You may have the gift of giving. A person in the Bible who exemplifies the gift of giving is Matthew. There are several reasons that I believe Matthew had this gift. First, he has more to say in general about giving than any other New Testament writer. Second, he offers more wise counsel about giving, and he is the only one who makes the statement that our giving should be done in secret. And third, he is the one who addresses the issue of *misuse* of money and resources.

Matthew was a tax collector, so he was familiar with money and financial transactions. He is the gospel writer who knows from personal experience a great deal about money and whether it is being used righteously or unrighteously. Matthew is the one who gives us the details about the gifts brought to Jesus. He is the one who records Jesus' condemnation of the Pharisees for allowing people to avoid caring for their parents financially, and who tells us about what the Pharisees did with the thirty pieces of silver that Judas returned to them after he had betrayed Jesus. As you look at the Gospel of Matthew, you will find a great deal of information about money, finances, material possessions, and the proper use of our resources.

At the outset of our discussion about giving, let me make three general statements about giving.

1. We are to give, regardless of our situation in life. Giving is not a ministry or motivational gift that is limited to those who are wealthy. A person's financial status has nothing to do with the motivational gift of giving. The person with this gift will desire to give regardless of the size of his bank account or the amount of possessions he has; the person with this gift will delight in giving and will find great satisfaction in giving.

2. All of us are commanded to give, and to do so with liberality. All believers are to give tithes faithfully and be generous in their offerings. The person with the gift of giving, however, "lives to give." This person can't help but give at every opportunity—he is quick to give as much as he can as often as he can. We must never leave the giving to those who have this gift. Each of us is to give as God commands.

3. Giving is not limited to money. A gift may be one of material resources, time, talent, energy, or creativity. The gift, however, will be one that has value and which produces or conveys a material benefit. The giver may volunteer time and talent and energy to a particular cause, knowing that his effort will produce a tangible blessing to others. Again, we all are to give in a multitude of ways, but the person with the motivational gift of giving is eager to give in every way possible.

But this I say: He who sows sparingly will also reap sparingly, and he who sows bountifully will also reap bountifully.

—2 Corinthians 9:6

71

᪥ What does it mean to sow sparingly? To sow bountifully? How can a person know whether his gift is sparing or bountiful?

᪥ Why does Paul use a metaphor of planting and harvesting on the topic of giving? How is giving similar to gardening?

Characteristics of the Gift of Giving

The ministry gift of giving has the following ten distinct characteristics:

1. The person with a gift of giving has a keen ability to make wise investments and purchases in order to have more money to give. Many people are bargain hunters and wise investors. The person with the gift of giving, however, seeks to save and to invest *in order to have more to give.* Many bargain hunters desire to save money so that they can spend the savings on themselves; the person who is a giver desires to spend the savings on the work of the Lord.

Read the parable that Jesus taught in Matthew 25:14–30, and note especially verse 29:

> For to everyone who has, more will be given, and he will have abundance; but from him who does not have, even what he has will be taken away.

❧ Explain this principle in your own words. Why does God bless those who have abundance in the context of this parable? Why does He take away from those who don't invest what He has given?

❧ How do you handle "extra money" when you have it? What is your motivation for saving or spending?

2. The person with the gift of giving has a desire to give quietly, not calling attention to himself. Persons with a gift of giving are not motivated by applause or public recognition. They find their satisfaction in making the gift. In fact, their total emphasis is on meeting the need, not on having others acknowledge that they have met the need.

> "Take heed that you do not do your charitable deeds before men, to be seen by them. Otherwise you have no reward from your Father in heaven. Therefore, when you do a charitable deed, do not sound a trumpet before you as the hypocrites do in the synagogues and in the streets, that they may have glory from men. Assuredly, I say to you, they have their reward. But when you do a charitable deed, do not let your left hand know

what your right hand is doing, that your charitable deed may be in secret; and your Father who sees in secret will Himself reward you openly.

—Matthew 6:1–4

⮜ What does it mean to do charitable deeds "before men"? Why does God not reward those deeds?

⮜ What does it mean to not left your left hand know what your right hand is doing? How is this done?

3. Those with this gift often do not respond to great pressure to give or to ardent appeals by professional fund-raisers. They want to give out of their own inner motivation, not from outward pressure. They are turned off by high-pressure tactics. They often respond readily, however, to simple requests from those who obviously are in need. Again, it is Matthew who recorded these words of Jesus: "Give to him who asks you, and from him who wants to borrow from you do not turn away" (Matt. 5:42).

4. The person with the gift of giving is usually eager to motivate others to give. The person desires so greatly to see a need met that he will challenge others around him—regardless of their financial situation—to give what they can. The person also knows the value of giving, that there is a cycle to giving that includes receiving. The giving-receiving-giving-receiving cycle is motivating and rewarding, and the person with the gift of giving knows this cycle personally and desires that others experience it.

5. The person with the gift of giving often has an ability to see financial and material needs that others overlook. He is quick to calculate how much is needed, when it will be needed, and how resources might best be applied to meeting the need.

6. The person with the gift of giving often judges others on the basis of their giving. He regards stewardship over material possessions and finances as indicative of a person's ability to be a good steward of spiritual matters. He takes to heart the teaching of Jesus:

> He who is faithful in what is least is faithful also in much; and he who is unjust in what is least is unjust also in much. Therefore if you have not been faithful in the unrighteous mammon [money], who will commit to your trust the true riches? And if you have not been faithful in what is another man's, who will give you what is your own?
>
> —Luke 16:10–12

Givers are very concerned about good stewardship, so they may live frugally and modestly—even if they have great financial wealth. Generous givers are often unrecognized because they are unpretentious in what they possess and use. They are not motivated to accumulate things, but rather to use things to benefit others. They desire to gain wealth only so that they can give away as much as possible in their lifetime.

⁓ In the verses from Luke 16 above, what are the "true riches" that Jesus was referring to? How are these riches different from the world's riches?

⁓ How does a person's faithfulness in little things indicate what he'll do with important things? Give practical examples of this principle.

7. The person with the gift of giving rejoices when his giving is an answer to someone else's prayer. Those with this gift delight in being the tools that the Lord has used. They rejoice because they have assurance that they heard correctly from the Lord. They rejoice that a legitimate need has been met. They rejoice that the faith of another person has been activated and built up. The person with a gift of giving always wants to be right on target when it comes to sensing needs and responding as the Lord leads.

8. The person with the gift of giving relies upon the wise counsel of his spouse. Those with this gift are so concerned about being good stewards that they look for confirmation that they are acting in obedience to the Lord. If the Lord is leading one godly person to meet a need, He will likewise deal with the godly spouse about the gift.

9. The person with the gift of giving desires to give gifts of high quality.
He does not look for the cheapest or most meager way to meet a need.
Rather, the giver wants to give in abundance and quality, just as the
Lord has given to him in abundance and quality.

**10. Persons with the gift of giving take joy in being a part of the ministry
of the person to whom they have given.** When a giver makes a material gift, he feels as if he is giving part of himself. He feels personally
invested in the ministry or the life of the person to whom he has given.
Being part of another person's success brings the giver joy.

> So let each one give as he purposes in his heart, not grudgingly
> or of necessity; for God loves a cheerful giver.
>
> —2 Corinthians 9:7

When have you received a gift that was given grudgingly? How
did the giver's attitude influence your perception of the gift?

When have you received a costly gift that was given cheerful-
ly? How did the giver's joy influence your perception of the gift?

Words of Caution to the Giver

Givers must guard against these tendencies:

They must never become so overly concerned with material goods that they neglect the spiritual dimension of their lives.

They must never attempt to control the ministry or life of another person through their gifts. At times, those who give are concerned with making certain that their gift is used in a proper way. Those who give must release their gifts to the work of God and trust others to manage and administer them.

They must never pressure others to give as generously as they do. Just as the people with this gift reject high-pressure tactics, so they must be careful not to engage in high-pressure tactics themselves.

They must never become stingy to their own families. Those who are intensely concerned about the needs of others often overlook the needs of their spouses and children. Legitimate needs of family members should be met.

They must always remember to be thankful for what they receive. Givers are often so focused on their own giving that they either rebuff or fail to acknowledge the things that they are given by others.

Heal the sick, cleanse the lepers, raise the dead, cast out demons. Freely you have received, freely give.

—Matthew 10:8

🔊 Notice that the preceding list of gifts does not include money. How can a person with the gift of giving bless others without spending money?

🔊 What gifts has the Lord given you, both spiritually and materially? How can you demonstrate your gratitude for those gifts?

The Behaviors of the Godly Giver

People with the gift of giving will be known by these characteristics:

   Thrifty: they will spend their money wisely, not wasting resources that could otherwise be used for ministry purposes.

   Resourceful: they will find a way to meet a need, either through their own giving or by motivating the giving of others.

   Contented: they will be content with what they have.

   Punctual: they recognize that it is better to meet a need quickly than to allow it to grow into an even greater need that will require even greater resources.

   Tolerant: they demonstrate a "give and take" in areas where others find it difficult to be flexible.

○○○ **Cautious:** they carefully research their investments and the ministries to which they give so that they are certain to use their resources wisely.

○○○ **Thankful:** they appreciate what they have and are grateful when they are used by God to meet a need.

Command those who are rich in this present age not to be haughty, nor to trust in uncertain riches but in the living God, who gives us richly all things to enjoy. Let them do good, that they be rich in good works, ready to give, willing to share, storing up for themselves a good foundation for the time to come, that they may lay hold on eternal life.

—1 Timothy 6:17–19

∾ What might cause a wealthy person to become haughty? How does this attitude demonstrate faulty thinking, according to these verses?

∾ Good works do not bring salvation, so what was Paul referring to when he said, "that they may lay hold on eternal life"? How is godly giving a way of holding onto things of eternity?

Jesus: Our Role Model for Giving

Jesus, of course, is our role model for sacrificial, joyful giving. No person has ever given as Jesus gave, for He gave His very life on the cross so that you and I might have eternal life. Jesus taught His disciples, "Greater love has no one than this, than to lay down one's life for his friends" (John 15:13). Jesus willingly gave His life in obedience to His father. Perhaps the most famous verse in the entire New Testament is about giving: "For God so loved the world that He gave His only begotten Son, that whoever believes in Him should not perish but have everlasting life" (John 3:16).

The person who has the gift of giving has a tremendous opportunity to be a blessing to others in the Body of Christ, to encourage others in the proper use of their finances, and to make the extension of the gospel possible.

For where your treasure is, there your heart will be also.

—Luke 12:34

∽ Give real-life examples of when you've seen this principle at work. Why does a person's treasure Influence his or her heart?

🙠 Where is your treasure? What do you value most in life? How is this influencing your daily decisions and actions?

🙠 Today and Tomorrow 🙠

TODAY: ALL CHRISTIANS ARE CALLED TO GIVE GENEROUSLY, BUT THE GIFT OF GIVING ENABLES A PERSON TO MEET NEEDS THAT OTHERWISE WOULD BE MISSED.

TOMORROW: I WILL LOOK FOR OPPORTUNITIES THIS WEEK TO MEET THE NEEDS OF OTHERS, AS THE LORD LEADS.

LESSON 8

The Gift of Organization

---------------- ❧ **In This Lesson** ☙ ----------------

LEARNING: IF CHRIST IS THE HEAD OF THE CHURCH, WHY DO WE NEED
GIFTED LEADERS?

GROWING: HOW CAN A PERSON RECOGNIZE THE GIFT OF LEADERSHIP?

☙

Are you uncomfortable in a leaderless group? Do you feel restless or frustrated if things seem to be disorderly? You may have the motivational gift of organization. This gift is sometimes called the gift of leading, ruling, or the gift of administration. The Greek word literally means "the one who stands out front."

The person who has the gift of organization is frequently misunderstood. Often, this gift is not perceived as being a matter solely of human will. We must never lose sight that God, our heavenly Father, created the universe, including us human beings, with a strong sense of order. God created in a very precise, sequential, and organized manner. The laws of nature are extremely practical in their application, and yet they are unseen laws. Issues of authority and headship are deeply rooted in the spiritual realm. And last but not least, the church was designed by God to function with order, with all gifts of the Holy Spirit exercised in an orderly way.

The person with the gift of organization is no less spiritual than those who bear any of the other ministry gifts. In fact, to the Christian all things are spiritual. There is no distinction before God between secular life and spiritual life—*all* of life is spiritual. Everything has a spiritual foundation. The person who is given the motivational gift of organization is given a degree of insight into what God is doing and desires to be done. The person with this gift might be called a "spiritual dreamer in action"—a person who can see the intended design of God and turn it into reality. He has the capacity to see what God is doing in the spiritual realm and how God desires to bring about spiritual results in the physical realm, and he understands immediately how to engage in a major undertaking to turn the will of God into a reality on earth. He has an ability to visualize the final result that God desires.

A person in the New Testament who exhibits the ministry gift of organization is James. One of the main criticisms of James is that he is too practical and not spiritual enough—he emphasizes works as being of equal importance to faith. We must not misunderstand James: he regards faith very highly and sees no substitute for it. But he is very concerned that faith be put to work in an orderly and effective way.

> Therefore, to him who knows to do good and does not do it, to him it is sin.
>
> —James 4:17

✎ When have you known that something needed to be done, but you chose not to do it? What was the result? How is such an omission a sin?

84

☙ How might a person with the gift of leadership help others to avoid such sins of omission? How might a gifted leader have helped you in the previously mentioned situation?

Orderly and Effective Works

Throughout the epistle of James, we find a strong admonition that we should be "doers of the word and not hearers only" (James 1:22). In fact, James says that, if we are hearers only and not doers, we have deceived ourselves. As you read through the verses from James below, note his great practical concern for orderliness and diligence.

> For if anyone is a hearer of the word and not a doer, he is like a man observing his natural face in a mirror; for he observes himself, goes away, and immediately forgets what kind of man he was. But he who looks into the perfect law of liberty and continues in it, and is not a forgetful hearer but a doer of the work, this one will be blessed in what he does.
>
> —James 1:23–25

☙ When have you been unaware of something embarrassing on your face or clothing? How did you feel when you discovered it?

❧ Now suppose that you had seen the embarrassing situation in a mirror, but failed to fix it. In what ways is that a good picture of knowing God's Word but failing to put it into practice?

> If a brother or sister is naked and destitute of daily food, and one of you says to them, "Depart in peace, be warmed and filled," but you do not give them the things which are needed for the body, what does it profit? Thus also faith by itself, if it does not have works, is dead.
>
> —James 2:15–17

❧ When have you known of someone else's desperate need but failed to do anything about it? When has that happened to you?

❧ In what sense can faith be "dead"? Why is practical application of God's Word essential in keeping faith alive?

How might a person with the gift of leadership be helpful to other Christians in the above situation?

A Picture of Order in the Early Church

James was the leader of the church in Jerusalem, frequently referred to as the "first church." Early in the formation of the church, problems arose in the distribution of food. Many of the believers had pooled their earthly resources and were meeting together daily for fellowship, for study of the Word, and for eating meals. Some were being neglected while others were indulging themselves. As you read below what happened, note how organization was linked to spiritual concerns, and how organization created a climate in which spiritual fruit was produced.

Then the twelve summoned the multitude of the disciples and said, "It is not desirable that we should leave the word of God and serve tables. Therefore, brethren, seek out from among you seven men of good reputation, full of the Holy Spirit and wisdom, whom we may appoint over this business; but we will give ourselves continually to prayer and to the ministry of the word."

And the saying pleased the whole multitude. And they chose Stephen, a man full of faith and the Holy Spirit, and Philip, Prochorus, Nicanor, Timon, Parmenas, and Nicolas, a proselyte from Antioch, whom they set before the apostles; and when they had prayed, they laid hands on them.

Then the word of God spread, and the number of the disciples multiplied greatly in Jerusalem, and a great many of the priests were obedient to the faith.

—Acts 6:2–7

Organization is not counterproductive to the work of the Holy Spirit in a group. Rather, the Holy Spirit desires order. When the ministry gift of organization is strong and Spirit-led in a group, all other ministry gifts flourish. The gospel is preached, souls are saved, and the church grows and develops even greater strength.

What motivated the twelve apostles to find people with the gift of organization? How did Stephen and others help the twelve to carry out their own ministries more effectively?

What sort of things did Stephen and the others do for the body of Christ? What did their gift of organization look like, in practical terms?

Characteristics of the Gift of Organization

The person who has the gift of organization bears the following twelve characteristics.

1. Those with the gift of organization have an ability to see the "big picture." They have a capacity to dream big and to believe that God desires to do something more than presently exists.

2. Those with the gift of organization have an ability to break down large projects into bite-sized pieces. They are able to break down long-range goals into a sequence of short-range goals.

3. Those with the gift of organization are self-starters. They are highly motivated to accomplish the goals that are before them. They take great joy in seeing the pieces of the larger puzzle fall into place one by one

4. Those with the gift of organization are keenly aware of all the resources necessary for accomplishing a goal. The minute that this person sees the goal which God sets before him, he begins to analyze all that is necessary for accomplishing the goal, and he begins to envision ways that the resources might be acquired.

〜 How good are you at seeing "the big picture" concerning long-term projects? How do you react when someone else gets into the "nitty gritty details" of a project?

~ Do you tend to be a self-starter, or do you prefer to follow the lead of others? How quick are you to analyze what will be required to accomplish a goal?

5. Those with the gift of organization are confident that God-given goals can be accomplished. They are can-do people, and they have very little tolerance for those with objections, unfounded concerns, and a negative or pessimistic outlook.

6. Those with the gift of organization know how to delegate. They know that they can't do it all, and they are willing to relinquish both authority and responsibility so that others can be successful in understanding and completing part of the larger goal. They know how to seek out the right people to undertake various parts of the task that lies ahead.

7. Those with the gift of organization often have little tolerance for details. Too many details can bog down the person who has the gift of organization.

8. Those with the gift of organization are able to receive criticism without crumbling. As mentioned earlier, the literal meaning of the Greek word for ruling or leading is "the one who stands out front." The person who is out front is on the firing line—he is the one most likely to be criticized, questioned, blamed, and misunderstood. He has to have skin as thick as a rhinoceros. If he is to accomplish God's plan, he must not allow criticism to deter him or slow him down.

9. The person with the gift of organization needs to know that his co-workers are loyal to him and committed to the task at hand. The person who leads expects loyalty—not only to himself, but to God. The person with this gift is so loyal to God and so committed to obeying God that he has little tolerance for anyone who is disloyal or wavering in commitment.

10. Those with the gift of organization have a tendency to move into a leadership role if no leader emerges or if a situation becomes disorderly. They cannot sit idly on the sidelines if they perceive that nobody is moving into a leadership role. Because of this tendency, the person with this gift can sometimes be misinterpreted as being egotistical or too aggressive. In fact, the person is simply moving to establish order where he perceives disorder.

When have you been involved in a group that seemed to lack leadership? How did the lack of leadership effect the group as a whole? How did it effect you personally?

When have you seen someone arrive on the scene and confidently take the lead on a project? What gifts did that person have which made the project flow more smoothly?

11. Those with the gift of organization want to see a goal reached as quickly as possible, as well as possible, and with as few resources as possible. They abhor wasting time, money, talent, or energy.

12. Those with the gift of organization delight in seeing projects accomplished. They are not motivated by making money, working with people, or receiving applause for the finished job—rather, they are motivated by seeing the task accomplished in a way that is pleasing to God. They need few rewards other than the deep satisfaction in knowing that God is pleased and that good work has been done.

> Having then gifts differing according to the grace that is given to us, let us use them: . . . he who teaches, in teaching; . . . he who gives, with liberality; he who leads, with diligence. . . .
>
> —Romans 12:6–8

🔖 Why is diligence necessary in utilizing the gift of leadership? In what sense is it the equivalent of the giver who gives with liberality? The teacher who teaches?

🔖 Why are all these gifts listed together? Why isn't the gift of leadership listed first? How might a gifted leader tend to forget this fact?

Warnings to Those wth the Gift of Organization

The person who has the motivational gift of organization must be aware of these negative tendencies:

⌐ **Never taking time to rest or reflect:** Those with this gift are rarely without a project to do. As soon as they complete one project, they are eager to move on to the next one. None of us was created to be all work and no play. God made the Sabbath for man to rest physically, emotionally, and spiritually—to relax in His presence and allow God to rejuvenate us from the inside out.

⌐ **Driving others beyond the limits of their abilities:** The person with a gift of organization is so highly motivated to complete a task that he might drive others without regard for their capacity, other commitments, or personal limitations. They must be sensitive to the fact that others may not be as motivated, energetic, or insightful as they are.

⌐ **Relying on their own abilities rather than trusting God to guide priorities:** Those with this motivational gift are usually so capable that they must guard against the tendency to run ahead of God's timetable or to fail to ask God often, "Are we doing what You want us to do? Are we doing this in the way that You want us to do it? Do we have our priorities straight?"

Come now, you who say, "Today or tomorrow we will go to such and such a city, spend a year there, buy and sell, and make a profit"; whereas you do not know what will happen tomorrow. For what is your life? It is even a vapor that appears for a little time and then vanishes away. Instead you ought to say, "If the Lord wills, we shall live and do this or that."

—James 4:13–15

❧ In what sense is a person's life like a vapor? In what sense does one's life have consequences that last forever?

❧ What is James' point in these verses? What attitude is he encouraging in all believers? How might this attitude be extra difficult for someone with the gift of leadership?

Behavior of the Godly Administrator

If you have been placed into an administrative or leadership role, develop the qualities of behavior listed below. If you desire to work effectively for a godly administrator or leader, look for these qualities to be manifested in a consistent manner:

- **Orderliness:** every aspect of life is subject to order.
- **Initiative:** no delay in taking action.
- **Responsibility:** willing to take responsibility for all aspects of a project or group endeavor.
- **Humility:** a recognition that others must be part of the team if the job is to be done quickly in the face of criticism.
- **Determination:** knowing that the goal is worthy of the price which must be paid for the job to get done.
- **Loyalty:** to God and to others in authority, as well as to those who are following his leadership

A godly leader regards himself as under the authority of the Holy Spirit, and he is a joy to work with and for! An ungodly leader is a tyrant to be avoided.

> Who is wise and understanding among you? Let him show by good conduct that his works are done in the meekness of wisdom.

> —James 3:13

∽ What is meekness? How is it characterized in a person's life? In what ways is true wisdom meek?

∽ Why is such meekness necessary in a godly leader? How does this contradict the wisdom of the world concerning effective leadership?

Jesus: The Head of the Church

Paul has this to say about Jesus as the One who orders all things in His church:

And He put all things under His feet, and gave Him to be head over all things to the church, which is His body, the fullness of Him who fills all in all.

—Ephesians 1:22, 23

Jesus referred to Himself as the Shepherd of His flock. He organized His disciples by choosing twelve and then sending them out two by two. Jesus was certainly delegating authority when He gave His disciples this commandment: "Go into all the world and preach the gospel to every creature" (Mark 16:15). As with all the ministry gifts, Jesus is our role model for the proper use of the gift of organization. We all are to be orderly in the way that we conduct our lives, but the people with this ministry gift find great satisfaction in being organized and in seeing work done, tasks accomplished, and projects completed. They enjoy work and are likely to be working every day of their lives.

&. Give some examples of godly leadership from the life and ministry of Jesus. What principles of leadership can you glean from His example?

&. When was Jesus also a follower? What can all Christians learn from His example about being a godly follower?

✿ Today and Tomorrow ✿

TODAY: A GODLY LEADER IS FIRST AND FOREMOST A GODLY FOLLOWER OF CHRIST.

TOMORROW: I WILL CONSCIOUSLY WORK AT BEING A GODLY FOLLOWER THIS WEEK, WHETHER OR NOT I HAVE THE GIFT OF LEADERSHIP.

✿ Notes and Prayer Requests: ✿

LESSON 9

The Gift of Mercy

❧ In This Lesson ❧

LEARNING: HOW IS THE GIFT OF MERCY DIFFERENT FROM LOVING OTHERS?

GROWING: WHAT ROLE DOES MERCY HAVE IN THE BODY OF CHRIST?

Do you have a real heart for people? Do you feel tenderness toward others? Do you look for ways of showing kindness? Do you have a desire to see people love one another to a greater degree? If so, you probably have the gift of mercy. One of the people who best exemplifies the gift of mercy in the New Testament is the apostle John.

One of the foremost characteristics of the person gifted with mercy is love, and of all the apostles John is the one who wrote the most about love: the love of God, the commandments of Jesus to love one another, and extensive admonitions to the early believers about love. John valued love highly and often referred to himself as "the one whom Jesus loved." To have been loved by Jesus was the highest reward and the most meaningful mark of identification that John felt he could claim for himself.

Very often, men think that mercy is a feminine gift. It is neither feminine nor masculine; it is a character quality that every believer is to manifest. The person who is gifted with mercy often seems tough on the outside, but is very tenderhearted and kind on the inside. John was not the least bit effeminate—he was referred to by Jesus as a "son of thunder." Yet John was tenderhearted and merciful.

The person who bears this gift of mercy is a source of joy in any body of believers—he is the one that everyone enjoys having around and is eager to see. And we can readily understand why, for who fails to respond to unconditional love and mercy?

> If someone says, "I love God," and hates his brother, he is a liar; for he who does not love his brother whom he has seen, how can he love God whom he has not seen? And this commandment we have from Him: that he who loves God must love his brother also.
>
> —1 John 4:20, 21

☙ What does it mean to love your brother? Who is your brother? What sort of love is referred to here?

☙ In what sense is it a lie to say you love God if you don't also love your brother? Why can't a person love others without loving God first?

John's Focus on Love in the Church

John wrote a great deal about the need for love in the Body of Christ. As you read through the verses below, notice that John always saw love as an action, not as an emotion only. He always related love to Jesus Christ, who truly is our source of love. Without Jesus Christ, it is impossible for a person truly to love unconditionally.

> Beloved, let us love one another, for love is of God; and everyone who loves is born of God and knows God. He who does not love does not know God, for God is love. In this the love of God was manifested toward us, that God has sent His only begotten Son into the world, that we might live through Him. In this is love, not that we loved God, but that He loved us and sent His Son to be the propitiation for our sins. Beloved, if God so loved us, we also ought to love one another.
>
> —1 John 4:7–11

❧ How did God demonstrate His love for mankind? What would have been different if He had only loved emotionally, without putting it into action?

❧ In what sense is love the gift of God? What does this teach concerning the source of our love for one another? What is required to tap into that source?

Characteristics of the Gift of Mercy

The motivational gift of mercy has a number of outstanding qualities, including these seven characteristics:

1. Those with the gift of mercy have a great ability to feel the joy or distress of others. They have a heightened sense of discernment regarding emotions. They rarely have to ask, "How are you doing?", intuitively sensing how another person is doing emotionally. They are usually more concerned with inner hurts than with outer material or physical needs. They are especially drawn to those who are lonely, fearful, or troubled.

2. Those with a gift of mercy are able to identify with others and to vicariously experience what others are going through. They have a special empathy and understanding of those who are under emotional stress, and they are actively attracted to those individuals. They have a great desire to help others by their presence and friendship. They can "rejoice with those who rejoice, and weep with those who weep" (Rom. 12:15).

3. Those with a gift of mercy desire to alleviate hurt in others. They see virtually no benefit in pain, suffering, distress, or sorrow. They want to see all negative feelings healed and removed immediately. At times, they may clash with those who have the gift of exhortation, who are able to see benefit in suffering. The person who has the gift of mercy must be willing to allow the gift of exhortation to function fully, just as the person with the gift of exhortation must be patient and kind toward the person who has a gift of mercy. Those with other ministry gifts may reach out to hurting individuals with words and material blessing, but the person with the gift of mercy is likely to reach out with open arms.

4. Those with the gift of mercy are very sensitive to statements and actions that may hurt others. They intuitively feel the pain on behalf of others. They often react harshly if their friends or family members are rejected or hurt in any way. They may respond in a defensive and even angry way if they sense that a person is doing something that may injure someone they love. They are very sensitive to criticism of others.

5. Those with the gift of mercy have an ability to sense unconditional love and to detect expressions of love that are insincere or hypocritical. They have a greater ability to be wounded themselves; they are highly vulnerable to feeling emotional pain. Part of the merciful person's ability to empathize with another person's pain grows out of his own experience.

6. Those with a gift of mercy have a great need for friendship. They need to be in relationships that are marked by commitment and steadfastness. They do not have a high tolerance, however, for friends who manifest a critical spirit.

7. Those with the gift of mercy are reluctant to speak against any person, regardless of what they have done. The danger, of course, is that they may not speak up in times when they *should* confront evil. Mercy must always be balanced with justice. God is always merciful, but it is equally true that God is always just.

Let all bitterness, wrath, anger, clamor, and evil speaking be put away from you, with all malice. And be kind to one another, tenderhearted, forgiving one another, even as God in Christ forgave you.

—Ephesians 4:31, 32

 Define the following terms, giving examples of each.

Bitterness:

Wrath:

Clamor:

Evil Speaking:

Malice:

 What does it mean to be tenderhearted? How is this done? Give practical examples of it.

Warnings to Those Gifted in Mercy

The person who is gifted in mercy must continually guard against these tendencies:

Being too emotional to the point of losing sight of the greater purposes of God. The person with a gift of mercy must always maintain an objective awareness that God's purposes and God's methods are higher than those of men, and that God may at times break a person in order to refashion him.

Being weak and indecisive. The person with this gift has a tendency to express tenderness and acceptance rather than firmness and resoluteness for the truth of God and righteous behavior. The merciful person must choose to stand strong in the face of evil.

Being too quick to draw conclusions in defense of those who are being criticized or hurt. Those with this gift must not be too impulsive in showing mercy.

Being too forward in their desire to minister to others with their presence, forgiveness, and kindness. Those with this gift must be sensitive to know when they are too close for another person's comfort.

Failing to note when acts of mercy and unconditional love cross an invisible line and become expressions of sexual desire. Those with the gift of mercy are wise to extend their gift to those of the same sex. The gift of mercy is rooted in love, and it is very difficult for some people to maintain proper bounds when showing mercy to those of the opposite sex. At times, those who receive mercy from a person of the opposite sex misinterpret their acts of mercy as acts of romantic love.

Therefore, as the elect of God, holy and beloved, put on tender mercies, kindness, humility, meekness, longsuffering; bearing with one another, and forgiving one another, if anyone has a complaint against another; even as Christ forgave you, so you also must do. But above all these things put on love, which is the bond of perfection.

—Colossians 3:12–14

Define the following terms, giving examples of each.

Tender mercies:

Humility:

Meekness:

Longsuffering:

Notice that the qualities of love listed in these verses are all associated with forgiving others. Why is this Paul's focus concerning love? What does this teach about the gift of mercy?

The Godly Expression of Mercy

The person with a gift of mercy is known by these traits:

- **Attentive:** watchful over those who are in need or trouble of any kind.
- **Sensitive:** aware of needs in others even without them saying anything.
- **Fair:** desiring impartiality and fairness.
- **Compassionate:** feeling the hurts of others, as if they were their own.
- **Gentle:** soft-spoken, tender, and caring.
- **Yielding:** willing to give way to the wishes of others so that harmony and peace might prevail in a person's heart.
- **Sacrificial:** willing to suffer if it will help another person.

As we have said for each of the motivational gifts, we are all called to bear the fruit of the Spirit, and gentleness is one of the character traits identified as fruit in Galatians 5:22, 23. The person who has the ministry gift of mercy does not have to say to himself, "I should be merciful in this situation. I must speak kind words and deal with this person gently." Rather, the response of mercy and kindness is immediate and automatic. The person with this ministry gift actually seeks out those who are hurting so that he might show mercy. Nothing is as fulfilling to a person with this gift as having the opportunity to listen to and comfort another person who is hurting. Nothing is as important as defending the person who seems to be outcast, downtrodden, or treated unfairly.

> But love your enemies, do good, and lend, hoping for nothing in return; and your reward will be great, and you will be sons of the Most High. For He is kind to the unthankful and evil. Therefore be merciful, just as your Father also is merciful.
>
> —Luke 6:35, 36

❧ How do these verses apply to a person with the gift of mercy? How do they apply to all Christians, regardless of spiritual gifts?

❧ When have you been unthankful toward God? How has He demonstrated kindness to you just the same? How can this help you exercise the gift of mercy toward others?

Jesus—Our Role Model for Mercy and Love

Jesus was the embodiment of God's Love. He was God's "only begotten son," sent to this world as an expression of God's infinite love for mankind. Jesus always acted in a merciful, loving way to people in need. He saw and responded to inner needs as much as to outer material or physical needs. His desire and goal was that mankind should be reconciled to God the Father and experience God's forgiveness and unconditional love.

John wrote about Jesus and love: "By this we know love, because He laid down His life for us. And we also ought to lay down our lives for the brethren" (1 John 3:16). John also wrote, "For God did not send His Son into the world to condemn the world, but that the world through

Him might be saved" (John 3:17). Jesus did not merely talk about or command others to love; He expressed love and gave love in the most generous and merciful way: He gave His very life for the sins of the world.

> Therefore be imitators of God as dear children. And walk in love, as Christ also has loved us and given Himself for us, an offering and a sacrifice to God for a sweet-smelling aroma.
>
> —Ephesians 5:1, 2

🔊 Why did Paul command us to be imitators "as dear children"? How does a child imitate his father? How can this help you imitate God's love?

🔊 What does it mean to "walk in love"? How is this done? How is "walking" more active and deliberate than "standing"? How does this relate to loving others?

A Much-Needed Gift in the Church

In any body of believers, there are likely to be more people who feel that they have a gift of mercy than any other ministry gift—and I believe that is healthy for the church. If the church is to be a family, then love, kindness, tenderness, forgiveness, and mercy must be freely flowing. Any body of believers that is characterized by mercy is going to be healthy. Those who show mercy are going to provide a spiritually helpful balance to those who have other ministry gifts.

Very often, God puts us into marriage unions and business partnerships with those who have a balancing gift to the one that we have. The gift of mercy certainly balances several of the other gifts. It is the supreme balance for the gift of prophecy. In situations in which prophets may wound with their sharp denunciation of evil and their strong call to righteousness, the person with a gift of mercy is needed to "bandage" the wounded.

When any of us are being tempted or are undergoing a difficult period, we long for those who will show mercy to us. We need the tenderness and love which they show.

Love has been perfected among us in this: that we may have boldness in the day of judgment; because as He is, so are we in this world. There is no fear in love; but perfect love casts out fear, because fear involves torment. But he who fears has not been made perfect in love. We love Him because He first loved us.

—1 John 4:17–19

What does it mean to have boldness in the day of judgment? How does love provide this boldness? How might this boldness influence one's exercise of the gift of mercy?

How does perfect love cast out fear? What role does God's love for us play in this process?

Today and Tomorrow

TODAY: ALL CHRISTIANS ARE CALLED TO LOVE ONE ANOTHER, BUT THE GIFT OF MERCY GOES THE EXTRA MILE IN THAT LOVE.

TOMORROW: I WILL ASK THE LORD TO HELP ME LOVE OTHERS MORE SELFLESSLY THIS WEEK, AND SEEK TO SHOW MERCY TO THOSE WHO NEED IT.

Developing Your Motivational Gift

Once you have identified your motivational ministry gift, you have a responsibility before God and to others to *develop* your gift. The ministry gift that you have been given by God is subject to your will for its operation—you must *choose* to use it. The Holy Spirit wants you to use your motivational gift at all times, and always for the benefit of the church.

An Aspect of Christ's Nature

Only Jesus Christ embodied all seven of the motivational gifts. As we have pointed out throughout these lessons, Jesus truly was the Prophet, Servant, Teacher, Exhorter, Giver, Leader, and Merciful One. The motivational gifts as a whole are a portrait of Jesus in action on earth and in our lives today through the ministry of the Holy Spirit.

Each of us has been given the privilege of manifesting one facet of our Lord's ministry as a point of emphasis in our lives. It is as we work together bringing Christ to the world that we function as His *body*—the full manifestation of Christ that is capable of leading people to reconciliation with the Father, making disciples, and teaching by word and example what it means to be a Christian.

> Give no offense . . . just as I also please all men in all things, not seeking my own profit, but the profit of many, that they may be saved. Imitate me, just as I also imitate Christ.

> —1 Corinthians 10:32—11:1

❱ How did Jesus' life and ministry illustrate these verses? How did Paul imitate His example?

❱ What did Paul mean when he said that he pleased all men in all things? How was this different from following the teachings of the world?

Moving Beyond Your Own Ministry Gift

A faithfulness to one's own motivational gift does not mean that we cannot step into other ministry roles. For example, let us assume that people are required to direct the parking for a church so that parking is orderly and the church services can begin promptly. Helping to park cars is a ministry that is often undertaken joyfully and successfully by those who have the motivational gift of service. Let us further assume, however, that your particular gift is exhortation. Helping with the parking lot is not a ministry to which you would gravitate, or in which you would find satisfaction week after week. But on any given Sunday, should there be a lack of people to help with this ministry, you certainly would be capable of assisting in it.

The Holy Spirit will help each of us to function outside of our motivational gift *if the need arises.* On the whole, however, a person is going to find the greatest satisfaction, fulfillment, and success when he operates within his motivational gift. It would be both presumptuous and prideful to say to another person, "Oh, I can't help you with that urgent need right now—that isn't my ministry gift." When crises arise, the Holy Spirit's grace can help any believer to respond effectively as long as we are willing to be used and empowered by the Spirit.

If you are gifted as a teacher, however, it would be wise of you to say, "Oh, yes, I can teach Sunday school this year," and unwise for you to say, "Yes, I'll take on the responsibilities of organizing the ministry to those who are homebound or in nursing homes." The person gifted in teaching will find fulfillment as a teacher. He may be capable of leading the nursing-home ministry, but he will not find that work fulfilling, and he will not be as effective or satisfied in the role as a person who is gifted in organization.

Using this same example, we must also recognize that it would be an act of disobedience to the Lord for a person gifted as a teacher to decline a teaching opportunity out of rebellion, false humility, or misplaced priorities. The Lord has given us our motivational gifts for us to *use* them, and He will always present ample opportunities for us to use them so that we might grow in them and bless others. Be open to the ways in which the Holy Spirit may lead you into opportunities to use your gifts, even though you may be a bit fearful or concerned about how well you may do in the ministry role presented to you. This is a natural response, even if you are gifted in a particular area. Say yes to the Lord and then trust the Holy Spirit to help you use your gift to the best of your ability.

> All things are lawful for me, but not all things are helpful; all things are lawful for me, but not all things edify. Let no one seek his own, but each one the other's well-being.
>
> —1 Corinthians 10:23, 24

✎ What is the main purpose of the motivational gifts, according to these verses? How can a person know when his gifts are being used correctly?

✎ How might these verses apply in situations of special needs, such as the parking lot illustration above?

What About Manifesting the Fruit and Gifts of the Spirit?

We are to manifest the ministry of Jesus Christ to the world, and part of this means that believers should bear the likeness of the Holy Spirit into the world. The fruit of the Spirit is to become our character as we employ our ministry gifts (see Gal. 5:22, 23). Furthermore, we should be willing at all times to manifest any and all of the gifts of the Holy Spirit should He desire to use us for His ministry purposes.

We are to be clean and pure vessels through which the Holy Spirit might pour His power, love, wisdom, and assistance. The spiritual gifts, often called the "gifts of the Spirit"—such as those identified in 1 Corinthians 12:8–10—belong to the Holy Spirit and are identified by the apostle Paul as being given by the Holy Spirit. They are aspects of the Holy Spirit's own power that He imparts to believers on occasion in order for the believer to minister more effectively to others. In the operation of these spiritual gifts, it is the Holy Spirit that provides the motivation or inspiration to the believer to act in a specific way at a specific time and for a specific purpose. As the believer is obedient to the Holy Spirit and allows the Holy Spirit to work through him, he acts *as Jesus would act* toward meeting the need in another person's life.

These spiritual gifts are not innate in the believer; they reside in the Holy Spirit. They are not for the benefit of the believer through whom they function; they are for the benefit of another person who is experiencing need or trouble. They should bring no glory to the person who manifests them; all praise and honor should be given to God from whom they flow.

The difference between these spiritual gifts and the motivational gifts is that the spiritual gifts in 1 Corinthians 12:8–10 reside in the Holy Spirit, and they operate totally at the will of the Spirit. The motivational gifts reside in us—imparted to us on a permanent basis by the Holy Spirit at the time of our acceptance of Jesus Christ as Savior—and they are never removed from our lives. They operate to a great extent as we will them to operate—in other words, as we develop them and choose to use them.

There are diversities of gifts, but the same Spirit. There are differences of ministries, but the same Lord. And there are diversities of activities, but it is the same God who works all in all. But the manifestation of the Spirit is given to each one for the profit of all.

—1 Corinthians 12:4–7

🙠 In what ways are your arms gifted differently from your teeth? What is the purpose for the specific roles of your many body parts? What is required to keep those gifts functioning?

🙠 How does this metaphor apply to the various gifts of the Spirit?

Developing Your Spiritual Gifts

The development of your spiritual gifts begins with an act of faith in the Lord Jesus Christ that He can and will work through you. We must be obedient first to what we know is true about God the Father, Jesus Christ, and the work of the Holy Spirit. As James wrote, "Be doers of the word, and not hearers only" (James 1:22).

We are prepared and made ready for service as we turn from sin and disobedience, and choose to believe in Jesus Christ, trust God in all things, and obey God's commandments and the leading of the Holy Spirit. The Holy Spirit indwells you as a believer, and He will prepare you and empower you for ministry. And at that point, our faith and obedience will *compel* us to use our gift; we find that we cannot *not* act.

> But in a great house there are not only vessels of gold and silver, but also of wood and clay, some for honor and some for dishonor. Therefore if anyone cleanses himself from the latter, he will be a vessel for honor, sanctified and useful for the Master, prepared for every good work.
>
> —2 Timothy 2:20, 21

☙ What is a "vessel for honor"? How is it different from a vessel used for dishonorable purposes? Give some real-life examples of each.

☙ What are the spiritual parallels that Paul was alluding to in these verses? What is required of a Christian if he is to be fit for the use of the Holy Spirit?

Once we have a full understanding that Jesus Christ can and does work through us, we are called to develop our ministry gift in these four ways:

1. We must choose to walk in the Holy Spirit daily. We must examine our own lives, repent of our willful pride in choosing to do things our way, and intentionally yield control of our lives to the Holy Spirit. We must give God permission to work in us and through us. We must ask for the help and guidance of the Holy Spirit on a daily basis. We must be sensitive at all times to the opportunities that the Holy Spirit is putting in our path.

> I say then: Walk in the Spirit, and you shall not fulfill the lust of the flesh.
>
> —Galatians 5:16

What does it mean to "walk in the Spirit"? How is this done on a daily basis?

What is "the lust of the flesh"? How is its fulfillment the opposite of walking in the Spirit?

2. We must learn all we can about the characteristics of our particular ministry gift. Our prayer should continually be, "Lord, help me to understand this precious gift that You have given me and to know how best to develop it and use it." The best source for learning about your particular motivational gift is the Word of God. Study the lives of those who seem to embody your particular ministry gift. Read everything that Jesus had to say about your gift. Read what Paul, John, and others in the New Testament wrote about the employment of your gift. Grow in your understanding of how God wants you to use your gift.

> All Scripture is given by inspiration of God, and is profitable for doctrine, for reproof, for correction, for instruction in righteousness, that the man of God may be complete, thoroughly equipped for every good work.
>
> —2 Timothy 3:16, 17

Define the following in your own words:

Doctrine:

Reproof:

Correction:

Instruction:

What role does the Bible play in these things? What role does the Holy Spirit play? What role do you play?

3. We must focus on the development of our gift. Focus on the gift that you have been given. Run the race that the Lord has put before you, and run with diligence, focus, and patience (see Heb. 12:1). Run with a single-minded goal of becoming an expert contributor of your ministry gift to the Body of Christ, with your eyes continually on the Lord and on His desires (see 1 Cor. 9:24). Put aside any distractions and refuse to take any detours. Readjust your priorities so that your number-one emphasis is on the godly use of your ministry gift in as many situations as possible—at home, on the job, in the community, and especially in your church.

> Do you not know that those who run in a race all run, but one receives the prize? Run in such a way that you may obtain it. And everyone who competes for the prize is temperate in all things. Now they do it to obtain a perishable crown, but we for an imperishable crown.
>
> —1 Corinthians 9:24, 25

How does an athlete "run in such a way" that he obtains first prize? What is involved?

What does it mean to be "temperate in all things"?

4. We must get involved in a ministry and use our gift to the best of our ability. Motivational gifts are developed through use. Find a ministry about which you care deeply and offer your services (your gift). Get involved. The more you use your gift, the stronger you will become in it, the more effective you will be, and the greater benefit you will render to the Body of Christ. Paul wrote that we are to be like athletes in training when it comes to the exercise of our ministry gift. A good training program requires regular and consistent effort. So, too, the employment of our motivational gifts. We must get involved and stay involved.

Called to Bear Fruit

Jesus called His disciples to bear fruit—"much fruit" (see John 15:8). It is in our fruitfulness that Jesus Christ is expressed to the world and the Father is glorified. You will become fruitful as you trust God to work in your life, and as your learn to walk day by day in the Spirit, learning all that you can about your ministry gift, focusing on its development, and using it at every opportunity. In fact, you cannot *help* but be fruitful, because it is the Holy Spirit who will be producing fruit in you and through you. He is the life that is surging though the Vine into you as the "branch," and He will bear fruit. As Jesus taught,

> Abide in Me, and I in you. As the branch cannot bear fruit of itself, unless it abides in the vine, neither can you, unless you abide in Me. I am the vine, you are the branches. He who abides in Me, and I in him, bears much fruit; for without Me you can do nothing.
>
> —John 15:4, 5

Choose to abide in the Lord and be obedient to His call on your life—it is a call to minister in His name and for His glory. Be true to the motivational ministry gift that He has given you.

🙠 What does it mean to abide in Christ? How is this done?

🙠 Why is this abiding necessary when using motivational gifts? What happens when we try to use our gifts apart from Christ?

Do Try This at Home!

The motivational gifts are designed to be used *together* to build up the church. We must recognize that the church is not a building or an organization—it is a living spiritual entity, a body composed of all people who believe in the Lord Jesus Christ as the Son of God and the Savior sent by God to reconcile mankind to Himself. Genuine "chruch members" are wherever you find believers in Jesus Christ. Sometimes that will be at work, or in the community as a whole.

Your ministry gift is to function in *all* settings, not merely when you are serving on a church committee or as a part of a church-sponsored program. Whatever your gift may be, find ways to employ it in love, humility, and peace to those around you, and in conjunction with other members of the Body of Christ.

You and your spouse are likely to have different ministry gifts. Openly acknowledge your differences and find ways in which you can work together, building up one another and your family rather than tearing one another down through criticism or competition. You and your children may very well have different ministry gifts. Again, openly acknowledge your gift and seek ways of employing them in a harmonious way that builds up your family life.

Our ministry gifts are intended to bring glory to God. Make that your goal always. Exercise your ministry gift as you believe the Lord Jesus Christ would manifest it; do what He would do and say what He would say. And always, use your ministry gift with the fullness of the character of the Holy Spirit: "love, joy, peace, longsuffering, kindness, goodness, faithfulness, gentleness, and self-control" (Gal. 5:22, 23). If you use your gift while manifesting the true character of our Lord, you *will* be a blessing to others, and you will reap the Lord's rewards and blessings in return.

> Therefore I remind you to stir up the gift of God which is in you through the laying on of my hands. For God has not given us a spirit of fear, but of power and of love and of a sound mind.
>
> —2 Timothy 1:6, 7

What does it mean to "stir up the gift of God which is in you"? How is this done? Why does it need to be stirred up?

How can fear interfere with your use of God's gifts? What role is played by "a sound mind" in eradicating such fear? How is it done?

Today and Tomorrow

TODAY: GOD HAS GIVEN ME A GIFT WHICH IS VITAL TO THE HEALTH OF HIS BODY.

TOMORROW: I WILL ASK HIM THIS WEEK TO TEACH ME HOW TO USE MY GIFT TO HIS GLORY.